CELEBRITY CHEFS

Giada De Laurentiis

Jeanne Nagle

Enslow Publishing
101 W. 23rd Street
Suite 240
New York, NY 10011
USA

enslow.com

Published in 2017 by Enslow Publishing, LLC
101 W. 23rd Street, Suite 240, New York, NY 10011

Library of Congress Cataloging-in-Publication Data
Names: Nagle, Jeanne, author.
Title: Giada De Laurentiis / Jeanne Nagle.
Other titles: Celebrity chefs.
Description: New York, NY : Enslow Publishing, 2017. | "2017 | Series: Celebrity chefs | Includes bibliographical references and index.
Identifiers: LCCN 2016003316 | ISBN 9780766077591 (library bound)
Subjects: LCSH: De Laurentiis, Giada—Juvenile literature. | Celebrity chefs—United States—Biography—Juvenile literature. | Cooks—United States—Biography—Juvenile literature.
Classification: LCC TX649.D4 G53 2017 | DDC 641.5092—dc23
LC record available at http://lccn.loc.gov/2016003316

Printed in the United States of America

To Our Readers: We have done our best to make sure all website addresses in this book were active and appropriate when we went to press. However, the author and the publisher have no control over and assume no liability for the material available on those websites or on any websites they may link to. Any comments or suggestions can be sent by e-mail to customerservice@enslow.com.

Photo Credits: Cover, p. 1 Jason LaVeris/Getty Images; star icon throughout book Yulia Glam/Shutterstock.com; p. 4 Ilya S. Savenok/Getty Images; p. 7 Andy Cross/Getty Images; p. 10 Sara De Marco/Shutterstock.com; p. 11 Ton Koene/picture-alliance/dpa/© AP Images; p. 15 John M. Heller/Getty Images; p. 16 Mariordo (Mario Roberto Duran Ortiz)/File:Paris_06_2012_Cordon_Bleu_3149.jpg/Wikimedia Commons; p. 17 Rob Loud/Getty Images; p. 19 Donato Sardella/WireImage/Getty Images; p. 23 Ethan Miller/Getty Images; p. 27 Lester Cohen/WireImage/Getty Images; p. 28 Neilson Barnard/Getty Images; p. 30 Gustavo Caballero/Getty Images; p. 35 Richard Drew/© AP Images; p. 37 Amy Sussman/Getty Images; p. 38 PR NEWSWIRE/© AP Images; p. 40 Tasia Wells/FilmMagic/Getty Images; p. 43 Jon Kopaloff/FilmMagic/Getty Images; p. 45 ZIMMERMAN PAUL/SIPA/Newscom; p. 48 Noam Galai/FilmMagic/Getty Images; p. 52 Alexander Tamargo/Getty Images; p. 54 Ethan Miller/Getty Images; p. 59 Jeffrey Mayer/WireImage/Getty Images; p. 60 Stefanie Keenan/Getty Images; p. 66 Caroline M. Facella/WireImage/Getty Images; p. 67 Neilson Barnard/Getty Images; p. 70 Bryan Chan/Los Angeles Times/Getty Images; p. 72 Directphoto Collection/Alamy Stock Photo; p. 76 MIGUEL MEDINA/AFP/Getty Images; p. 78 Bob Riha Jr/WireImage/Getty Images; p. 79 Manny Hernandez/Getty Images; p. 81 Jason LaVeris/FilmMagic/Getty Images; p. 85 John Parra/WireImage/Getty Images; p. 88 Bob Fila/Chicago Tribune/MCT/Getty Images; p. 92 zhekoss/Shutterstock.com; p. 93 lsantilli/Shutterstock.com; p. 95 Solutioning Incorporated/Shutterstock.com; p. 97 al1962/Shutterstock.com; p. 99 Niki Crucillo/Shutterstock.com; p. 101 zi3000/Shutterstock.com; p. 102 al1962/Shutterstock.com; p. 104 foodlove/Shutterstock.com; p. 106 Olga Nayashkova/Shutterstock.com; p. 108 Lesya Dolyuk/Shutterstock.com; p. 110 tomertu/Shutterstock.com.

CONTENTS

Giada De Laurentiis has one of the most highly recognizable faces on The Food Network.

Film and
Food

Giada De Laurentiis comes from a family that, for generations, has had two driving passions: movies and food. Considering these facts, perhaps it does not seem surprising that she ended up becoming a celebrity chef, cooking in front of audiences via the magic of television.

Giada Pamela De Benedetti was born on August 22, 1970, in Rome, Italy. She is the oldest child of actress Veronica De Laurentiis and producer Alex De Benedetti. Her grandfather was film producer Dino De Laurentiis, who produced popular and Oscar-winning films in Italy and the United States. Most of his notable movies were released between 1950 and 1980. His first wife, Giada's maternal grandmother, was Italian film actress Silvana Mangano.

Giada started cooking as a young child. She remembers her first time in the kitchen as a five-year-old chef, helping her mother make pizza dough. "I would move the flour around to make a well, and then I'd break the eggs and put them in the middle, and my mom would slowly put in the flour and salt," she recalled in a 2009 interview with *Redbook* magazine.[1]

Another favorite childhood memory was having a dish prepared for her on special occasions. One of her favorite dishes was rigatoni pasta in béchamel, or white cream sauce. While she certainly enjoyed the pasta, she says the best part of the dish was the melted crust of cheese on top. "For my birthday, I got to pick the top off," she recalled in a 2008 magazine interview. "Then my brother and sister would say, 'This is disgusting, we don't want to eat it anymore.'"[2]

Italian Roots in America

The family lived in Italy for the first few years of Giada's life. When she was eight years old, her parents divorced. She and her siblings (brothers Igor and Dino and sister Eloisa) took their mother's last name and moved with her to the United States. Veronica De Laurentiis and her children first made a home in New York City but soon moved to Los Angeles, where her father had relocated to make movies in Hollywood.

Celebrities visited often. Actor Arnold Schwarzenegger and director David Lynch were frequent dinner guests. Giada remembers playing hide-and-seek with a young Drew Barrymore.[3]

The De Laurentiis household definitely was a hot spot for food, with or without celebrity guests. Every Sunday the various members of her mother's side of the family would gather to cook huge meals. Giada remembers those weekends as being filled with noise, good cooking, and loved ones.

"In my Italian family, there has always been a passion for fresh food and for tradition and the value that's put on cooking and how that brings a family together," she told a reporter in 2013.[4]

Giada enjoys teaching others about food and how to prepare it. Her energy excites food lovers and cooks alike, especially when she talks about food from her native Italy.

Little Miss
⭐ Manners

Mealtimes at Giada's house were not just an opportunity for the family to connect. The De Laurentiis children were also taught how to behave around the dinner table. "My family took manners very seriously," she once told a reporter from *People* magazine. Among the lessons the children practiced and learned were how to carry on a polite conversation with people seated nearby and, of course, how to chew with their mouths closed. She also recalled being required to tuck books underneath each armpit while handling silverware, in order to learn how to use a knife and fork appropriately.[5]

Trouble Adjusting

Being surrounded by a close-knit family and hanging out with movie stars was pretty much a dream childhood for Giada. But outside of her home, things were not always easy or fun. A self-described shy child, Giada had major problems fitting in at school when she first came to the United States. She did not speak a word of English when she arrived. While she was learning the language, she did not get as much practice as was needed, since she was expected to speak Italian at home. Because she had trouble communicating and understanding what was going on in the classroom, she wound up, in her

8

words, "flunking" first grade. Having to repeat the grade had a long-lasting impact on her. With a hint of regret in her voice, she told a *New York Times* podcast audience that she "ended up being the oldest person in every grade until I graduated."[6]

Not speaking the language was not the only thing that made Giada different in the eyes of her classmates. Even her name, which means "jade" in Italian, set her apart. She was not blond with blue eyes, as so many of the children in Southern California seemed to be. She used to bring lunches to school that the other kids thought were weird. Her lunch box might easily contain spaghetti Bolognese left over from dinner the night before. Bringing more common lunch items did not help, either. Instead of bologna sandwiches, she brought mortadella, a type of Italian cold cut similar to bologna. Replacing peanut butter was Nutella, a chocolate-hazelnut spread that, back in the 1970s, was popular in Italy but not in the United States.

Odd Girl Out

Being different does not have to be a bad thing, but in young Giada's case, it was. For the most part, her classmates avoided her because she was not more like them. She often ate lunch alone, or sometimes with a sympathetic teacher. Giada remembers sitting in the back of the school bus "because kids wouldn't want to talk to me."[7] (Of course, since she had trouble mastering English, for a while the other children literally could not talk to her.)

Complicating matters was the fact that Giada developed as a young woman at a fairly young age. "I developed breasts when I was nine years old," she shared with a reporter in 2011, "and I was the only one in my class. I would literally sit in class hunched over because I was so embarrassed about my body."[8]

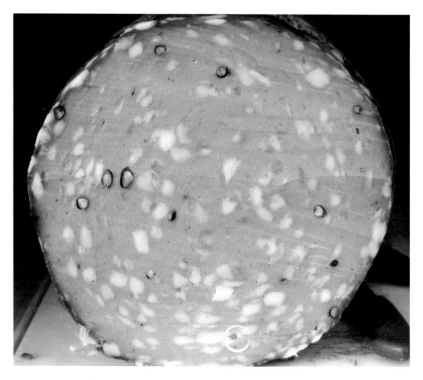

Mortadella is an Italian cold cut, or salumi, that is similar to American bologna. However, it often has nuts, chunks of fat, and spices dotted throughout the pork. Many children that Giada went to school with found her lunches strange and stayed away from her.

Being ignored and avoided was not even the worst of it. Giada also felt bullied at school. She has said that kids in her class would tease her and call her names. As she remembers the situation, some of her teachers did nothing when this happened. Others, however, tried to give her tips on how to get along better with her classmates.

At Home With Food

One way that Giada found comfort from her troubles was to visit a food store that her grandfather had opened. Dino De Laurentiis had grown up selling pasta made by his parents in a factory in Naples, Italy. His interest in and passion for food never left him, even after he became a famous movie producer. To satisfy his desire to share the type of food he grew up with, he created DDL Foodshow in the 1980s. This was a combination market and restaurant that served gourmet Italian ingredients and prepared dishes. Giada loved everything that was sold in the store and was a big fan of food from Naples in general.

This food shop in Naples is very similar to the one Dino De Laurentiis created in the 1980s. Italian products (such as olive oil, spices, or vinegars), as well as olives, cured meats, and pasta were all for sale there.

★ Civil Food War

Each of Italy's twenty regions has its own claim to fame when it comes to food. The biggest divide in the country, however, is that between northern and southern Italian cooking. Giada's family is from the south, so her allegiance is clear. "[T]he south probably has the best food in the whole entire country," she told *Elle* magazine in 2014. "Northern Italian people will argue that point, but that is my personal opinion."

In that same article, she gave high marks to the cuisine of Sicily. "It is the freshest. It is the cleanest. It just has the most flavor pretty much everywhere in Italy."

She reserved her highest praise, however, for a dish born in her grandfather's home city. "Naples has the best pizza in the world," she said, "and I mean everywhere. You could go to a truck stop in Naples, and they have phenomenal pizza."[9]

Dino De Laurentiis brought chefs he knew in Italy over to the United States to cook for the store, which had locations in New York City and Los Angeles. Each store was equipped with a kitchen, complete with a pizza oven. Along with cooked dishes ready to eat, each DDL Foodshow location had an antipasti bar, which was set up like a salad bar. Antipasti are appetizers or "starters," such as olives, peppers, and sliced meats and cheeses.

Between the ages of twelve and fourteen, Giada used to hang out at the Los Angeles store. She has said she was amazed by how much people liked to come to the shop, not only for the food, but simply to listen to the Italian being spoken while dishes were being prepared and served. The things that made her different at school—speaking Italian and eating Italian food—were wholeheartedly welcomed by the store's customers. She also liked to watch the chefs preparing the food.

> *"Being in the kitchen—cooking or baking—just makes me feel good all around . . ."*

Beyond making her feel more at home, visiting DDL Foodshow gave Giada a glimpse into a possible future career. "It's where I realized that I wanted to be a chef," she told a *Parade* magazine reporter in 2014. "I didn't know if I could make money at it, but I loved it enough to try."[10]

Watching chefs work in the kitchen of her grandfather's place made Giada feel more comfortable with who she was. Actually cooking herself built up her self-confidence and even helped her win a few new friends at school. She once told a reporter, "I'd bring things to class that I'd cooked at home, and my classmates were like, 'Wow. This is amazing, and that girl with the funny name cooked it!'"[11]

Off to College

At first, Giada's family was not exactly thrilled with the idea of her becoming a professional chef. While food was very important to the family, movie-making was more so. Her mother was an actress, and her grandfather was a producer, as is her aunt Raffaella, known as Raffy. (Giada's siblings would wind up going into movie-making: Dino Alexander became a production assistant and apprentice editor, Eloisa became a makeup artist, and Igor did some acting.) It was sort of assumed that Giada would join the family business and somehow make a career in the film industry as well.

"My family made movies, so I always felt like if I wanted to be in front of the camera, I had every opportunity to do that," she told Julia Moskin of the *New York Times*. "I never had any interest."[12]

When she was a teenager, Aunt Raffy gave Giada a small part in one of her movies. Giada was not comfortable being an actress, and from then on she tried to stay away from the entertainment industry.[13]

Regardless of what career she pursued, it was decided that Giada had to continue her schooling after graduating from Marymount High School in Los Angeles. She was the first member of her family to attend college. She enrolled at the University of California at Los Angeles (UCLA) as an anthropology major.

During her time at UCLA, she met Todd Thompson, who would later become a designer for the Anthropologie chain of retail clothing stores. The two started dating when Giada was

Producers Martha De Laurentiis (far left), and Raff De Laurentiis participate in a discussion honoring Dino De Laurentiis along with directors Michael Mann (center), and Jonathan Mostow, as well as former California Governor Arnold Schwarzenegger.

nineteen years old. When she brought him home to meet the family, they teased her about Todd's table manners and habits. Giada recalls, ". . . my grandfather would say to me in Italian, 'Who is this person butchering his pasta by cutting it with a fork and knife?'"[14]

Planning for Paris

Four years of studying anthropology did not change Giada's feelings about becoming a professional chef. After she graduated from UCLA in 1996, she made a decision that was very bold, at least in the eyes of her family. Giada enrolled in the prestigious Le Cordon Bleu culinary school in Paris, France. This was quite a leap for a shy girl who had never been far away from her family before.

De Laurentiis was the commencement speaker for the anthropology department at UCLA in 2009.

Le Cordon Bleu in Paris, France, is one of the world's premiere culinary schools. Students learn about technique and ingredients, as well as the restaurant business. Unfortunately for Giada, however, the classes were all taught in French.

Her grandfather was not happy about her going away to school or her career choice. As Giada has said, Dino De Laurentiis came from a generation that believed women should be wives and mothers, staying at home and taking care of the household. And even if they did find work—his daughters worked in the movie business, after all—it should not be as a chef. He thought cooking professionally was a man's job. He particularly did not like the idea of Giada, who was quite petite, lugging around big, industrial-sized pots because it was not especially "glamorous."

In response to her grandfather's concerns, Giada was quoted as saying. "I figured, 'Well, why should that stop me? I can work just as hard as a man.' When you love to do something, you just do it."[15]

Giada was particularly close to her grandfather, Dino, with whom she credits her love of food and cooking.

Chapter 2

Step by Step,
Dish by Dish

Any chef in the world would consider him—or herself—lucky to receive an education at Le Cordon Bleu, established in Paris in 1895. The very name "Cordon Bleu" is synonymous with cooking excellence. Having this culinary school on a resume tends to impress restaurant owners looking to hire talented kitchen help. There are Le Cordon Bleu branch schools virtually around the globe, but the original school is the most widely recognized and respected.

Giada De Laurentiis was smart to apply to Le Cordon Bleu. She had to know that both the skills she would learn there and the name recognition of the school would take her far in her career as a chef. Yet she also had an ulterior motive, or hidden reason, for wanting to study the culinary arts in Paris.

"I had never lived away from home," she said in a 2007 episode of the Food Network (now Cooking Channel) show *Chefography*. "So I thought, 'This is my chance to sort of blossom and grow up, and move away from my family, and break out of that bubble, and fend for myself.'"[1]

Veronica De Laurentiis, Giada's mother, is very supportive of her daughter, but she also knew when to give her tough love.

Fake It 'Til You Make It

De Laurentiis was not only up for a personal challenge when she moved to France, but she was ready to push academic boundaries as well. At Le Cordon Bleu, she was enrolled in what was known as the Grand Diplôme program, which was the most demanding program available at the school. Students who earned this diploma would be qualified to become fine cuisine chefs and/or pastry chefs.

Unfortunately, De Laurentiis's enthusiasm for pursuing her dream dimmed soon after she started classes in Paris. "The first three months were hell," she once said about her time at the culinary school. "All I wanted to do was come home."[2]

The situation was eerily similar to what she had experienced in elementary and middle school. She did not know anyone in Paris and felt very alone. Additionally, she did not speak French, which was needed to communicate both inside and outside the classroom. She felt like an outsider all over again, only this time she was not able to turn to the safety and comfort of home and family. Making matters worse was the fact that the teachers at Le Cordon Bleu were very demanding. De Laurentiis later recalled that pots, pans, and food were thrown around the kitchen when something went wrong or a student made a mistake.

"There was still a lot of sexism there and because I was a small woman who people knew came from a famous family, I took a lot of abuse," she recalled in a 2014 interview with the *Toronto Star*.[3]

Things got so bad that De Laurentiis called her mother, crying, and told her that she wanted to return to Los Angeles. Her mother refused. In fact, she told De Laurentiis that if she came home before graduating, the family would no longer support her financially.[4] She could not live at home, and she would basically be on her own. Veronica De Laurentiis also told her daughter that she would never forgive herself if she did not finish what she had started.

Apparently that was exactly the push De Laurentiis needed. She decided to tough it out in Paris and wound up doing quite well in her classes. After a year and a half, she graduated from Le Cordon Bleu with the Grand Diplômc. Things were not exactly perfect after that, however. Chefs need to taste food a lot as they cook. De Laurentiis had gained fifteen pounds during her time as a culinary student in Paris.[5]

Blending and Mixing

At Le Cordon Bleu, De Laurentiis was trained primarily in classical French cooking. Her culinary roots, however, were firmly planted in Italy. The differences between these cuisines were not as vexing as they might appear. Le Cordon Bleu boasts that the school's students, particularly those with the Grand Diplôme, are more than capable of applying the French techniques they learn to any other style of cooking.[6] In addition, France and Italy have similar climates and therefore use similar ingredients in their cuisines. For instance, Roquefort is a kind of French cheese that is very similar to the Italian gorgonzola. In the United States, these are often categorized as blue cheeses.

That is precisely what De Laurentiis did, using the skills she learned at Cordon Bleu to create Italian specialties with a twist. In fact, as she proceeded through her career as a chef, mixing things up became a kind of trademark for her. She has said she was inspired by her mother. Veronica De Laurentiis did not have access to many ingredients she would have had in Rome to make authentic Italian dishes. So she improvised, using what she could find and adapting the recipes as she went along. "Her way of combining the best of the old world and the new has been the inspiration for many of the recipes I create now," Giada De Laurentiis once wrote.[7]

> *"[W]ith fantasy and imagination you always find the best way to cook."*

Kitchen Help

Upon returning to the United States, De Laurentiis moved in with her boyfriend, Todd, and got busy looking for work as a chef. The first professional job she landed was as a line, or assistant, chef for the fine dining room at the Ritz-Carlton hotel in nearby Marina del Ray. Working under a French head chef there, helping to create fine cuisine, must have made her feel as if she was back at Le Cordon Bleu—hopefully without pots and pans flying through the air. Next, De Laurentiis worked at the famous Beverly Hills restaurant Spago, co-owned and run by celebrity chef Wolfgang Puck. At Spago she was able to put her dessert skills to the test as an assistant pastry chef. De Laurentiis recalls that working at the restaurant was fun but stressful. Making desserts for eight hundred or more tables of customers a night was exhausting. Safety sometimes took a back seat to quick productivity. De Laurentiis has said she suffered innumerable injuries while preparing sweets and getting pastries out to the celebrities who frequented the Spago dining room.

After a few years, De Laurentiis began to suspect that the fast-paced life of a restaurant line chef was not the career for her. "I realized that as much as I love this I wasn't able to survive," she told an interviewer with Amazon.com in 2003. "I needed to find a way to make this something that I could do long term and not get burned out."[8]

She decided to strike out on her own and began working as a private chef, cooking meals for several different clients in and around Hollywood. The first client she booked was director and actor Ron Howard. She also cooked for Los Angeles decorator Marilyn Greenspan and her husband, Eric, who later became De Laurentiis's lawyer.

Being a private chef for the famous and well-to-do was not always as glamorous as it might have seemed. De Laurentiis remembers working for one family who happened to own a large dog. The dog apparently liked De Laurentiis, which meant

Wolfgang Puck was one of the first chefs to reach celebrity status. Puck owns several restaurants, as well as a line of cookware, appliances, and gourmet food products.

that it seemed to get "underfoot" quite a lot. One November, as she was carrying a tray loaded with a Thanksgiving turkey and all the trimmings into the dining room, she tripped over the dog. As she tells the story, food went flying all over the place, "[a]nd of course the dog got the turkey. I was so humiliated I just wanted to run out the door."[9]

Food Multitasking

Around this time, De Laurentiis created her own catering company, GDL Foods. Private chefs generally cook for individuals, couples, or families. Caterers prepare food and beverages for parties, meetings, or other large events. By adding catering to her chef's resume, De Laurentiis could increase the amount of money she made working for herself. She has described GDL Foods catering as being "very profitable," meaning it allowed her to earn a good living.[10]

Another way she added income was to work as a food stylist. This was a freelance job, meaning that she worked for various clients on a job-by-job basis. As a food stylist, she was in charge of making food look good so it could be photographed for magazines, cookbooks, and other publications. De Laurentiis started this line of work by assisting a friend who lived on the East Coast. Whenever this photographer/stylist had a job lined up on the West Coast, De Laurentiis would help her out and act as her assistant.

> *"When people ask me what the best restaurant in L.A. is, I say, 'Uh, my house.'"*

Food styling felt somewhat natural to De Laurentiis. It reminded her of being back in Paris at Le Cordon Bleu.[11] One of the things chefs are taught at the school is presentation, which means how the food looks on the plate. When cooking fine cuisine, especially for a restaurant, chefs must remember that how the food looks when it is served is just as important as how it tastes or smells. Many chefs say that clients eat first with their eyes, then their noses, and finally, with their mouths.

Being Discovered

Working with her friend, De Laurentiis managed to get some high profile food styling jobs. Her work appeared in publications such as *Martha Stewart Living* and *Food & Wine*. It was through her connections at the latter magazine that De Laurentiis got one of the biggest breaks of her career. The magazine was doing

Stylists to the
★ Rich and Creamy

Food styling is every bit an art form as the photography used to capture its results, or even cooking itself. This job is not as easy as simply photographing food. The idea behind food styling is to make edibles look delicious, so that people either want to buy certain ingredients, eat at a particular restaurant, or make a recipe on their own at home. To make this happen, stylists use certain tricks that are, frankly, inedible. Paint, oil, putty, and wax are just a few of the items used on food that is being photographed, to keep it in place and looking picture-perfect.

When she worked as a stylist, De Laurentiis used to cook the food that she was styling. Even if no extra phony ingredients are added to a styling shoot, there are certain tricks of the trade that she has used. For instance, in order to keep meat from shrinking or losing moisture, stylists might only partially cook it—leaving it cooked on the outside but raw on the inside.

25

an issue devoted to food and family. The editors knew about De Laurentiis's family and their passion for food. They asked her to write an article for the magazine, as well as cook and style photographs to go along with the text.

Coincidentally, Dino De Laurentiis was set to receive the Irving G. Thalberg Memorial Award for lifetime achievement at the Oscars around the same time as the special issue was set to hit newsstands. Giada De Laurentiis thought that writing the article would be another way to honor her grandfather. She also figured that the job might help kick-start a career in food styling, which was something she did only occasionally, and usually as an assistant. She viewed being a full-time stylist as "a little more glamorous than what I was doing at the time, which was schlepping and cooking all day long, and basically doing all the manual work myself."[12] So she readily accepted the assignment.

As it so happens, an executive with the Food Network, Bob Tuschman, happened to see that issue of *Food & Wine* and was impressed with what De Laurentiis had done. He approached her about the possibility of her starring in a cooking show on the network. At first that shy little girl De Laurentiis had been rose to the surface, and she hesitated. Just as she had rejected being in front of a movie camera for so many years, she decided she had no desire to become a celebrity chef on television.

Tuschman told her that he saw a star behind the shyness. He added that he thought her true nature came out through not only in what she had to say about food, as shown in the *Food & Wine* article, but also in how she gestured and the sparkle in her eye when she talked about food in person. In other words, he liked what he saw on her demo reel, which is the equivalent of a video audition. "He said that what he saw was a lot of

Giada still uses many of the skills she learned as a food stylist today at the events she hosts.

It's hard to imagine now, but there was a time when Giada felt insecure in front of a camera.

passion coming out in me," De Laurentiis recalled in a podcast interview.[13]

Eventually, De Laurentiis agreed and signed a contract with the Food Network. America's next celebrity chef was about to hit television screens across the country.

Chapter

3

Star of the
Small Screen

For a long time, Giada De Laurentiis had maintained that she had wanted to become a chef in order to share her passion for food and make people happy with her cooking—but from inside a kitchen, where she could work somewhat anonymously. "I think a lot of chefs choose this profession to do just that," she told *New York Times* reporter Janet Moskin in 2012. "I think they like to bring joy to people, and like to see how excited they are to eat their food, but they don't actually want to engage with them on a personal level."[1]

Be that as it may, in 2003, De Laurentiis found herself preparing to be launched as a Food Network cooking star, no matter how reluctantly.

"I never wanted to do anything in front of the camera," she acknowledged in a later interview, "... but somehow I ended up right there. My family thinks it's hilarious."[2]

And So It Begins

De Laurentiis's first television appearance occurred in April 2003 on the Food Network. The show was titled *Everyday*

Giada likes to have fun while she cooks and encourages others to do the same. Helping others appreciate food like she does is her favorite part of being a celebrity chef.

Italian, and the content of the half-hour program was reflected in the title. De Laurentiis wanted the show to be about food from her native Italy, with dishes that were fairly common in the culture and recipes that were easy to follow. In fact, many of the dishes she prepared on-camera were actual De Laurentiis family recipes that had been handed down for generations, or at least were based on the originals. She adapted several of her recipes to fit the audience, so that they included elements of her Southern California upbringing as well.

Her aunt Raffy, whom she has called her "cooking soul mate," helped De Laurentiis prepare. "She finds the recipes and we tweak them," she once revealed in an interview with *Self* magazine. "We've been doing that since I was a kid."[3]

Starring in her own television cooking show was not an easy transition for De Laurentiis. For one thing, she was nervous about upsetting her family, particularly Dino. Before the show first aired, her grandfather took her aside and expressed some concerns. At that time, the Food Network was only ten years old, and the elder De Laurentiis was not familiar with it. The concept seemed a bit cheap or common to him. Dino was concerned about protecting the family name and reputation.

"He said, 'I built a huge business, and we have a very respectable name. Are you going to just trash it by doing food television?'" she recalled. "So I was very nervous. I didn't think about anything else other than . . . how I was going to make my family proud."[4]

> **Everyday Italian** *was filmed in the kitchens of real-life homes that were rented for taping episodes.*

Rating Her Own Performance

Regardless of what the family thought, it turned out that De Laurentiis was her own worst critic regarding her first performances during the first season of *Everyday Italian*. "I was terrible," she confessed in a 2014 interview, "and so unhappy."[5]

Part of the problem stemmed from the fact that De Laurentiis was still shy. Being in front of television cameras was torture for her. Then there was the added pressure of having to talk to viewers while cooking. "Talking to other people while you're cooking, it doesn't come naturally. You're chopping, the timing is tricky, and then you have to explain it all and tell stories and be up," she has said.[6]

It also did not help that the people she was supposed to talk to were, for all intents and purposes, virtual. She was performing in front of a small television crew, instead of actual viewers or even a live audience. She was thrown by the fact that she got no feedback from the people behind the cameras. No one laughed at the little jokes she made or could taste and comment on the food she was preparing. Basically, she was completely on her own.

The "no response" situation was combined with ridiculously long work hours, where taping one episode could take almost an entire day. De Laurentiis wrapped the first season of the show feeling tired and discouraged.

Thankfully, she began to feel more at ease as the seasons rolled on, and by season three she felt that she was doing a pretty good job. She credits lightening up a little and simply enjoying what she was doing for the turnaround. Today, she is thankful that executives at Food Network gave her the time to get past her struggles and come into her own.[7]

That Time She Tried to Kill Matt Lauer

In 2006, De Laurentiis's popularity as a celebrity chef had reached new heights. No doubt drawn by her success on *Everyday Italian*, executives at NBC's *Today Show* tapped her to become a contributor during the show's coverage of the 2006 Winter Olympic Games—which just so happened to take place in her native Italy. She was part of a segment called "Today's Cucina," where chefs prepared Italian dishes. She has since become something of a regular contributing correspondent on the show.

For Better and
★ For Worse

Beginning a promising career as a celebrity chef was not the only life-changing event that De Laurentiis experienced in 2003. After more than a decade together, she and Todd Thompson got married, on May 25 of that year. Six months later, she and the family were mourning the loss of her brother, Dino Alexander De Laurentiis. The younger Dino, who had worked in the production end of the movie business, had been diagnosed with melanoma about one year before his death on November 23, 2003.

De Laurentiis had appeared as a guest on the *Today Show* before then. Typically, the cooking segments in which she had appeared went well. However, there was one occasion, which happened during her first live appearance on the show in 2003, that caused her some embarrassment and grief. She was cooking chicken breasts with a pesto sauce. Because her time on air was limited, she used an old food-styling trick of cooking some of the chicken only on the outside, to make the display product look good on camera. Inside the meat was raw.

Today cohost Matt Lauer was unaware that the plate of chicken on display for the cameras was basically uncooked. At the end of the segment, he came in for a taste but took a piece from the display plate. As De Laurentiis herself tells the story:

So he puts it in his mouth and realizes it's raw. It's basically just seared. The camera follows him into the kitchen, and he spits it out. And he comes back and says, "Are you trying to kill us here?" I almost died.[8]

Bashes and Getaways

Everyday Italian was so well received by television viewers that the Food Network decided to give De Laurentiis more airtime as the star or host of other shows. The series *Behind the Bash* premiered in October 2006. This show drew partly on De Laurentiis's experience as a caterer, as it took viewers behind the scenes at a number of various high-profile parties and celebrations. The focus was on the food but also on all the preparations that make for a professional, large-scale party. Most of the events featured on the show were held in California and the New York City area.

The series started with a look at what it took to pull together the Grammy's after party. Viewers were also treated to a look at catering and event preparation behind a movie premiere, the American Cancer Society's Dream Bash, a combination chocolate and fashion show, and the fortieth anniversary of the daytime drama *Days of Our Lives*, among others. And that was just over the course of season one. Season two of *Behind the Bash* ran for only half of the original season's fourteen episodes.

Debuting in 2007, *Giada's Weekend Getaways* took De Laurentiis to different cities for three days of sampling local favorite eateries and dishes in each. Along the way she also visited sites in each location and participated in various activities. The first season took viewers to cities that were popular tourist destinations across the United States. The second

Working as a food stylist, caterer, and personal chef has given Giada a unique perspective on planning and hosting an event.

season continued that trend but also went international with stops in cities such as Paris and London, as well as Bermuda and the Hawaiian island of Maui. The first run of this show ended in 2008, but it was also rerun on the Food Network's sister network, the Cooking Channel, years later.

Helping to Create New Food Stars

Also in 2007, De Laurentiis stepped outside her usual duties as star/host and joined the reality food show *The Next Food Network Star* during its third season on the air as a guest judge. The show pitted chef wannabes against each other to win the title mentioned in its name. Winners were also given a shot at hosting their own Food Network cooking show. De Laurentiis returned to the show in 2008 as a guest advisor to the cooking hopefuls.

Finally, in 2011, she became a full-fledged member of the show's cast, as a judge alongside chef Susie Fogelson, and the man who brought De Laurentiis to Food Network in the first place, Bob Tuschman. This was also the year that the show dropped the word "Next" from the title, becoming what is known today as simply *Food Network Star*. In 2012, the format of the show changed a bit, wherein the celebrity chefs became coaches, or mentors, instead of judges. A mentor is someone who teaches and gives advice.

No Place Like Home

By the spring of 2008, De Laurentiis had wrapped up her breakthrough series *Everyday Italian* and was working on a new hosting venture on the Food Network, *Giada at Home*. While *Everyday Italian* had focused almost exclusively on food and cooking, the new show was more personal, offering viewers a

Giada got to attend some very special events while hosting *Behind the Bash.*

---

peek into the life of its star in addition to a slew of wonderful recipes.[9]

De Laurentiis also began another new role in 2008—that of mother to Jade Marie De Laurentiis Thompson, born March 28. She and her husband had pretty much decided not to have children, and that decision was strengthened after she lost her brother, Dino. She did not want to form a close bond with anyone for fear of them being taken away. Losing her beloved brother was horribly painful, but she knew losing a child would

Alongside Bobby Flay and Alton Brown, Giada hosted *The Next Food Network Star*, which aimed to find, train, and produce the next celebrity chef on the television network.

be a million times worse. After a while, however, she changed her mind. "[A] few years later, I thought, 'If I never have a child, that might be the saddest thing for me,'" she told a reporter in 2009.[10]

After the birth of her daughter, De Laurentiis's private and professional lives began to overlap each other even more. For instance, in a later episode of *Food Network Star*, De Laurentiis told fellow coaches Flay and Alton Brown that she was grateful for the opportunity to mentor up-and-coming chefs. She said the experience had given her "good little takeaways," meaning useful methods or pieces of advice, to use while raising or "mentoring" her daughter in the future.[11]

Bits and Pieces

From time to time, De Laurentiis has appeared as a guest on other Food Network shows, most notably *Iron Chef America*. During a 2006 celebrity version of this cooking grudge-match show, De Laurentiis and Flay went up against Rachael Ray and Mario Batali. Ray and Batali were declared the winners of this particular matchup—a fact that supposedly is still a sore point for De Laurentiis to this day.[12]

Through the years, the Food Network also has aired a number of specials hosted by De Laurentiis in addition to her longer-running shows. Some have a holiday theme, such as *An Italian Christmas with Mario and Giada*, which she cohosted with Mario Batali in 2004, and 2015's *Giada's Holiday Handbook*. Also in 2015, the Food Network aired a thirteen-week summer series titled *Giada in Italy*. As the show's name indicates, De Laurentiis went to Italy to tape the short series, which focused on Italian traditions, food, and culture as seen through the eyes

Giada's daughter, Jade, often makes appearances with her mother. Giada brought Jade to a charity event for Alex's Lemonade Stand in 2015.

of a native.[13] The Food Network launched the new six-episode series *Giada Entertains* in January 2016.[14]

In a move that has given her more control over her television projects, De Laurentiis formed the production company Linguine Pictures in 2012. A production company pulls together all of the elements involved in producing (meaning creating and airing or performing) an entertainment show. Run by De Laurentiis and her partners, Anne and Dan Fox, Linguine Pictures has produced a number of De Laurentiis's shows, as well as the Cooking Channel's *Tripping Out with Alie and Georgia*.

Pretty, Talented

On television, De Laurentiis is known for her looks as much as for her cooking. In fact, one of the knocks against De Laurentiis when she first started appearing on the Food Network was that—believe it or not—she was too pretty to cook. Viewers wrote in asking why the network had hired a model to pretend that she was a chef. Even after she became well-known, and her credentials as a

"I think it's okay to cook and be sexy. Why not?"

Cordon Bleu–trained chef were recognized, people still criticized De Laurentiis for being too sexy on her shows.

A lot of people have commented negatively on her wardrobe. When she first started at the Food Network, television executives wanted her to dress somewhat conservatively like Martha Stewart, in button-down Oxford shirts. De Laurentiis argued that such shirts restricted her movement while cooking and made her look boxy. She won the right to chose her own wardrobe.[15] Many viewers have claimed that her shirts are cut

Giada's Cartoonish
Personality

As if hosting and guesting were not enough, De Laurentiis added voice acting to her celebrity resume. In 2009, she voiced the character of Paulette in an episode of the Disney Channel 's animated series, *Handy Manny*. The role was not much of a stretch: Paulette was the owner of a pizza parlor whose "automatic pizza rolling machine" needs assistance from *Handy Manny* and his magical tools. De Laurentiis voiced a character in the 2014 Disney animated short film *Pixie Hollow Bake Off*, which was even closer to home. She played a pixie named Gelata who was trying to win a baking competition. Perhaps De Laurentiis, who did not want to have anything to do with acting as a teenager and young adult, did not mind these assignments because she could duck behind animated personalities, no matter how similar they were to her.

very low and her dresses are too tight.

De Laurentiis seems to have taken such comments in stride. How she looks is simply a part of who she is. "Part of the sensuality of Italian food is a certain look. I'm lucky enough to have gotten that from my mother," she has said of her appearance. "But I would like respect, that's for sure."[16]

She has made mention of how difficult it can be to be a woman celebrity chef, operating in a field that tends to be dominated by men. Although more and more women are making

Giada has received a lot of criticism for being a sexy chef. But she refuses to let it change anything about her look or her attitude.

inroads in the culinary field, there still seems to be extra pressure placed on women in the professional kitchen. That was certainly the case for De Laurentiis as she was studying in Paris and when she first started working as a chef.

"Over the years, I've been able to gain respect from the male chefs in my community," she told a reporter in 2014, "but I had to work harder than anybody else to get it. I had to make food that was better than anybody else. I had to make choices that were smarter than everybody else."[17]

Chapter

4

Books and
Tables

De Laurentiis did not become a celebrity chef on the strength of her television appearances alone. Her appeal is largely based on the ability of home cooks to easily follow her recipes. It makes sense, then, for her to offer those recipes in a format that aspiring chefs can refer to again and again. Therefore, shortly after her earliest success on the Food Network, De Laurentiis began publishing cookbooks as well. Consequently, she and her culinary creations could be found in living rooms, via television, and on bookshelves across America.

Cookbooks did not represent De Laurentiis's only attempt at publishing. She also became a children's fiction author with a series of books that had a culinary adventure theme.

And then there is the achievement that many chefs dream of from the first time they tie on an apron. It took about a decade from when she began cooking in front of the cameras, but by 2014, De Laurentiis had opened her own restaurant.

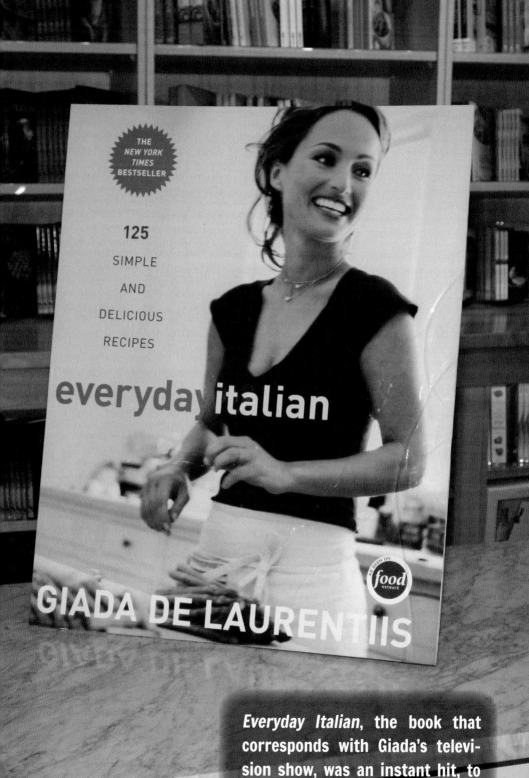

THE NEW YORK TIMES BESTSELLER

125
SIMPLE
AND
DELICIOUS
RECIPES

everyday italian

AS SEEN ON food network

GIADA DE LAURENTIIS

Everyday Italian, the book that corresponds with Giada's television show, was an instant hit, to the surprise of many.

Nice and Easy

The inspiration for De Laurentiis's first cookbook, *Everyday Italian*, was her television show of the same name. The book contained the same simple approach to cooking Italian dishes, with basic ingredients that were easy to find, as in the Food Network show. In all, De Laurentiis had included 125 recipes within its pages. The book landed in the No. 12 spot on the *New York Times* Best Seller list when it was first released in February 2005.

Initial reviews for the cookbook were lukewarm. *Publisher's Weekly,* a publication that provides information on the publishing industry as well as reviewing books, called it "a rather flat first effort."[1] Of course, a case could be made that the reviewer was missing the point of the book and De Laurentiis's overall style. For instance, noting that the book "lacks depth or meaning" was kind of silly, since the recipes were meant to be simple, basic, and easy to follow. The reviewer did admit, however, that *Everyday Italian* was a pretty good way for beginning cooks to learn about Italian cuisine and that ". . . De Laurentiis may be poised to be the next hot celebrity chef."[2]

Regardless of what reviewers thought, the public liked the cookbook quite a bit. De Laurentiis's publisher, Clarkson Potter, had only planned to print fewer than one hundred thousand copies of the book. They wanted to see how sales went before investing a lot of money in a book from a first-time writer. Sales took off like a rocket, and the publisher wound up printing more copies of the book five times, selling more than two hundred thousand copies within a month of its release.

The cookbook's sales figures got a boost on the front and back ends. *Glamour* magazine provided an excerpt, or sample, in its February 2005 issue, which acted as something of a preview of the book. After the book was published, De Laurentiis went on a tour of eighteen cities to promote it by signing copies and participating in cooking demonstrations. Both moves brought attention to the publication, which increased its sales.

Italian-American Cooking

De Laurentiis's second publishing effort, *Giada's Family Dinners*, was published in 2006. This cookbook showed off her ability to fuse culinary traditions from Italy and America. As David Kamp of *Vanity Fair* magazine noted, this could be something as simple as adding pancetta and chestnuts to a Thanksgiving stuffing made from Italian ciabatta bread, rather than white bread.[3]

By adding traditional Italian ingredients to the dishes featured in the book, De Laurentiis was trying to show that there is more to Italian cooking than red sauce and pasta. Her efforts to "Americanize" Italian dishes, so that they were easier to understand and cook, were not as successful—at least not according to her grandfather Dino.

"I did a recipe for meatballs with dark turkey meat and a little bit of ketchup," she told Kamp about the recipes in *Giada's Family Dinners*. "My grandfather wanted to die. He wanted to die!"[4]

Despite her grandfather's objections, the second cookbook turned out to be as popular as the first, if not more so. De Laurentiis's third cookbook, *Everyday Pasta*, arrived on store bookshelves the following year. While the emphasis of this book was, obviously, on pasta, De Laurentiis also included recipes for appetizers, salads, side dishes, and desserts that could make a full meal out of lasagna, ravioli, and the like. *Everyday Pasta* included a foreword by De Laurentiis that discussed her family's connection to pasta, explaining that her great grandparents were pasta makers back in Naples. She even gave a shout-out to her grandfather and to DDL Foodshow.

As with her first two cookbooks, *Everyday Pasta* found a spot on several best-seller lists, including that of the *New York Times*.

A Healthy Outlook

The publication of *Giada's Kitchen: New Italian Favorites* (2008), *Giada at Home: Family Recipes from Italy and California* (2010), and *Weeknights with Giada: Quick and Simple Recipes to Revamp Dinner* (2012) followed shortly after that. De Laurentiis had found a formula for writing cookbooks that not only was successful but also remained true to her style of cooking and living—simple and classic. She did not change much about her

Fans line up for hours in order to have De Laurentiis sign copies of her books.

authoring style until it came to cookbook number seven, *Giada's Feel Good Food* (2013). Even then, there was not a big difference in the ingredients used or the way the food was prepared. De Laurentiis simply intensified the emphasis on healthy eating and balance.

In her introduction, De Laurentiis told readers that this book was not meant to be a diet book. She didn't believe in diets, at least not for herself, because they were hard to stick to and tended to make people's weight go up and down with each failure or success of their diet plan. "I'm not a yo-yo and I can't put my mind or body through that," she wrote.[5] Instead, she offered recipes for food that fueled the body, not weighed it down, and she shared tips for healthy eating and exercise habits.

In November 2015, De Laurentiis released her eighth cookbook, *Happy Cooking: Make Every Meal Count . . . Without Stressing Out.* This book was, in many ways, a continuation of *Giada's Feel Good Food.* In addition to more quick and healthy recipes, the newer book included a year-long plan for staying fit and eating right. De Laurentiis emphasized yet again that everything in life, including food consumption, depends on maintaining balance. For the chef and author, that meant exercising and eating well but indulging in a guilty pleasure every now and again. De Laurentiis's cheats and treats usually involve chocolate in some way.

App and 'Net

Some of the material in *Happy Cooking* was adapted from a digital magazine De Laurentiis launched in 2013. *Giada: A Digital Weekly* was a subscription-based lifestyle and entertaining electronic publication distributed through a

Spit It Out, Giada!

As a celebrity, De Laurentiis has been subjected to gossip and a bunch of rumors. One of the craziest involved how a professional chef could manage to stay as fit and trim as she was. Supposedly someone on the crew at the Food Network anonymously revealed her secret: she used a spit bucket while taping her shows.

A representative for De Laurentiis said that they sometimes shoot multiple episodes a day and do multiple takes of scenes from each episode. If De Laurentiis ate during every take, she would make herself sick. So while she may actually chew and swallow only during a few takes, she absolutely does not spit food out into a bucket every time in order to avoid getting fat.

partnership with the publisher of the chef's first seven books, Clarkson Potter. The e-mag started life as an app, which received more than three hundred thousand downloads in its first year of availability. The popularity of the app convinced Clarkson Potter and De Laurentiis to offer the web-based version to an even wider audience.

Not all the content in the e-magazine was written by De Laurentiis. Instead, the material was gathered and presented by a team of trusted advisors, including family members, in consultation with the chef herself. These staffers tried to give subscribers an insider's look at De Laurentiis's life. De Laurentiis's main contribution was a self-written column on eating and living well. In addition to recipes, articles, and videos, the app offered an interactive "recipe box," which allowed readers to easily save or share meal instructions found in each issue.

Despite its initial popularity, *Giada Weekly* published its last issue on January 14, 2016.[6]

Cooking Up Adventures

While she was busy overseeing the launch of *Giada Weekly,* De Laurentiis was also working on a more traditional literary project—a series of children's books, written by the chef with author Taylor Morris, called *Recipe for Adventure.* The series focused on a young brother-sister team, Emilia and Alfie Bertolizzie, who are transported around the world courtesy of magical meals created by their aunt Zia. The first book in the series, *Naples!,* was published in 2013. Subsequent books, published in 2014 and 2015, took Emilia, Alfie, and readers to locations such as Paris, Hong Kong, New Orleans, Rio de Janeiro, Hawaii, and Miami.

More than a cookbook author, Giada also has a series of books about food adventures for children. The main characters of her series are based on her own family members.

The influences for the series characters were obvious to anyone who knew a bit about De Laurentiis's life story. Aunt Zia was based on Aunt Raffy, who appeared regularly on De Laurentiis's television shows and had been a cooking mentor to the chef since the latter was a little girl. Emilia was a fictional version of De Laurentiis herself, while Alfie was a stand-in for her younger brother Dino.

"We both had the bug of loving to cook and we were partners in it growing up together," De Laurentiis told reporter Jocelyn McClurg in 2013. "The books are sort of an homage to him."[7]

De Laurentiis has said that important themes in the books were family, friendship, and teamwork. "I wanted to give children the ability to travel in their minds and enjoy, accept, and understand what the different cultures have to offer," she said in a 2013 interview with *Instructor*, a magazine for educators now known as *Scholastic Teacher.*[8]

Opening Act in Vegas

In a 2012 interview with the *New York Times*'s Julia Moskin, De Laurentiis was asked if she was interested in opening a restaurant. She replied, "I think if you ask a lot of chefs they would say, 'If you don't need to do it, don't do it,'" adding that she might open a restaurant some day.[9]

Her hesitation was understandable. Owning and operating a restaurant is a huge undertaking, requiring a large investment of time and money on the part of a chef. As a working mother who hosted several television shows and specials, De Laurentiis was probably wondering if having her own eatery would be worth it.

However, when a prime location in Las Vegas, Nevada, became available about a year later, De Laurentiis decided to go for it. Construction on Giada started in May 2013, and the restaurant officially opened its doors in June 2014. De Laurentiis is one of the first female chefs to open a restaurant on the Vegas strip.

"I've noticed opportunities sometimes don't come to a woman in this business the way they do for men."

Located inside the Cromwell Hotel on the Las Vegas strip, Giada gives diners traditional Italian dishes and recipes for which De Laurentiis is known, such as lemon spaghetti with shrimp. The atmosphere combines homey comfort with Vegas

When Giada opened her first restaurant in 2014 many were skeptical of its success. It has proved, however, to be a popular dining destination in Las Vegas.

glitz, thanks to a clear view of the Bellagio Hotel's fountain across the street. There is also a photo booth in the lobby, so people who are waiting for a table can have their picture taken and uploaded directly to their Facebook accounts.

Pulling everything together for the grand opening was not easy. De Laurentiis had a hand in choosing everything from the chairs to the chandeliers that are etched with the chef's motto: "I eat a little bit of everything and not a lot of anything."[10] Two weeks before the restaurant was set to open, De Laurentiis fired her head chef. The opening went on as planned, even as she looked for a replacement chef.[11]

De Laurentiis joked with *Today* host Matt Lauer that opening the restaurant "has been a real labor of love, and sometimes it's been more labor than love."[12]

Chapter
5

Cooking for
Causes

Working for a cause can be a deeply personal experience. Most people choose to donate their time and money to organizations that mean something to them. Perhaps either they or someone they know has experienced a major life event or suffered an illness, so they choose to support an organization that makes life better for people in those situations. Maybe they have a special talent that can benefit an organization that is trying to solve a problem or offer assistance of some kind.

Giada De Laurentiis is no different in that regard. As a successful businesswoman, she has the means to offer financial support to any of a number of charitable organizations and causes. As a chef and culinary expert, she can cook for a group's fundraising events, offer to trade her cooking services for donations, or share her knowledge to help solve food related problems. Finally, as a celebrity, her involvement draws attention to a cause, thereby, it is hoped, increasing awareness, participation, and donations.

Over the years, De Laurentiis has lent her name, time, and money to several worthy charitable organizations and events. Among the causes she supports are two that are especially near and dear to her heart: cancer research and abolishing hunger.

Standing Up for Dino and Others

De Laurentiis was devastated when her brother Dino died from skin cancer in 2003, when he was only thirty-one years old. They were very close. The two talked daily and even lived next door to each other, which made it easy for them to practice cooking together. Giada De Laurentiis has described him as her rock. "He was the person I turned to for everything," she revealed to *Entertainment Tonight* in 2013.[1]

Largely in his honor, De Laurentiis has become a Stand Up To Cancer (SU2C) celebrity ambassador. In this capacity, she has talked about her family's experience with cancer and participated in fundraising and other events on the organization's behalf.

"I come from a place where I think life is never perfect. If we look deep inside, there are issues everywhere."

In 2013, De Laurentiis recorded public service announcements (PSAs) on melanoma and other skin cancers for SU2C and the Melanoma Research Association. The emphasis of the television and radio spots was on prevention and early detection. Dino Alexander's melanoma began as a mole smack dab in the middle of his back—a position that made it difficult to see. It came to his attention only after it started to bleed and would not stop.

"He immediately went into surgery, and from there it was all downhill," De Laurentiis was quoted as saying in a *Women's Health* interview.[2] The surgery did not help. The cancer metastasized, or spread throughout his body.

"Early detection can truly save your life," De Laurentiis said in a press release regarding the PSAs. "You don't have to die from melanoma or any other kind of skin cancer. My brother didn't have to die. Had we caught the melanoma early on, . . . he could have been cured."[3]

De Laurentiis has said that she does not usually do PSAs but made an exception in this case because of what her brother went through. "That experience woke me up. I realized we're all at risk."[4]

When Life Hands You Lemons...

De Laurentiis supports other organizations working to defeat cancer. Since 2010, she has volunteered to cook for a fundraising event for the Los Angeles chapter of Alex's Lemonade Stand. The charity, which helps children with cancer, was started by four-year-old cancer patient Alex Scott in 2000, when she opened a lemonade stand in her front yard to raise money to help find a cure. The national foundation started in honor of that first lemonade stand raises millions of dollars each year for childhood-cancer research and treatment efforts.

De Laurentiis has said that she admired Alex's fearlessness in the face of her disease, as well as her attempts to help herself and other children with cancer. "She did lose the battle in the end, but she won the support of so many people," De Laurentiis said during an interview regarding the 2013 edition of the L.A. chapter's fundraiser.[5]

The organization SU2C (Stand Up to Cancer) became very personal to Giada after having lost her brother to melanoma in 2003.

Giada wants to instill a sense of charity in her daughter, Jade. She also wants to instill a sense of fun! Here, they pose for photos at an event for Alex's Lemonade Stand in 2014.

Her work on behalf of Alex's Lemonade Stand goes beyond cooking for the L.A. chapter's annual fund-raising cookout. The charity also was featured on a 2012 episode of *Giada at Home*. "I just find that it makes me feel good, it makes me smile every day when I help out this charity," she said. "That, at the end of the day, is why we're all here: to give back and support each other."[6]

De Laurentiis also is an organizing committee member and regular attendee of The Pink Party in Los Angeles. This annual gala fund-raiser and fashion show supports the Women's Cancer Program at Cedars-Sinai Hospital at the Samuel Oschin

Comprehensive Cancer Institute. The program, which focuses on the ways in which cancer impacts women, provides clinical trials, research, and treatment plans. In 2014, she also served as the host of *Chef Challenge: The Ultimate Battle for a Cure*. This cooking-competition event helped raise money for women's cancer research at Mount Sinai Hospital in Toronto, Canada.

Battling Hunger With Ambassador Giada

De Laurentiis has said that after she gave birth to her daughter in 2008, her world view broadened quite a bit. She stopped thinking only of her time on Earth and began to envision what kind of world Jade and future generations would encounter. One factor that she could not tolerate, in the present or the future, was widespread poverty and the hunger and malnutrition that go along with it. So on "World Food Day" (October 16) in 2008, De Laurentiis became an ambassador for the international aid agency Oxfam America.

"In every nation on earth, people go to sleep hungry even though there's enough food on this planet to feed every woman, man, and child," said De Laurentiis at the time of her ambassadorship announcement. "I have joined Oxfam because it is a global organization that works to find long-lasting solutions to poverty around the world."[7]

As an ambassador, De Laurentiis has done more than simply give lip service to the Oxfam cause. Immediately following her becoming an Oxfam ambassador, she saw to it that inserts endorsing the organization were included in copies of *Giada's Kitchen* sold during her promotional tour for the cookbook. In 2009, she went a step further, spending a week with Oxfam staffers in Peru. There she witnessed firsthand how small-scale farmers struggle to put food on their own tables.

"I have brought back many stories from the villages I have visited," she said shortly after the trip was completed. "You really can't help but be moved by such amazing people. Now more than ever, I am convinced that we must invest more—and more wisely—in local agriculture to help poor farmers lift themselves out of poverty."[8]

Additionally, as she had regarding her work with Alex's Lemonade Stand, De Laurentiis prominently featured Oxfam in an episode of *Giada at Home*.

Beating Hunger With Teamwork

Another anti-hunger organization with which De Laurentiis has forged ties is Feeding America. Begun as a food distribution clearinghouse in Phoenix, Arizona, Feeding America has become one of the largest hunger-relief organizations in the United States, operating a vast network of food banks across the nation.

In 2007, pasta manufacturer Barilla teamed up with De Laurentiis and fellow celebrity chef Mario Batali to create *The Celebrity Pasta Lovers' Cookbook*, a collection of recipes available as a free download. Each time the cookbook was downloaded, Barilla donated one dollar, up to $100,000. De Laurentiis and Batali "reimagined" the favorite pasta recipes of several celebrities, including Harrison Ford and *Sex and the City*'s Kristin Davis. The two chefs also contributed tips on preparing pasta.

"Pasta is a favorite food among Americans, and celebrities are no exception," declared De Laurentiis in a press release promoting the effort. Added Batali, "Hunger relief in America is a challenge that requires constant attention and support, and who better to help address the issue than food producers and chefs?"[9]

Grow Your Own

When it comes to combating hunger and encouraging proper eating habits and nutrition, De Laurentiis has been known to get her hands dirty. In 2012, she helped create a "learning garden" at Foster Elementary School in Compton, CA. She was recruited as a volunteer by the organization The Kitchen Community, which helps connect kids to what they eat by providing the materials necessary to grow their own food in community gardens. Learning gardens have been established in several major US cities, including Chicago and Denver.

De Laurentiis worked alongside students, teachers, and members of the Compton community to create the Foster learning garden. The harvest of vegetables and herbs from the garden is used to cook dishes served in the school's cafeteria. De Laurentiis's Food Network biography page indicates that she has returned to Foster Elementary to check in on the student-gardeners and help maintain the school's garden.[10]

Support in the Kitchen

On numerous occasions, De Laurentiis has reached back to her catering roots and given culinary support to charity events hosted by other celebrities. Case in point is her participation in the Third Annual Block Party at the Grove, hosted by Tiger Woods. The event benefited the Tiger Woods Learning Center, which helps train low-income students in the STEM (science, technology, engineering, and math) disciplines. De Laurentiis prepared a four-course gourmet meal for the 2007 Block Party event. In addition to fillet mignon and crab, the menu for the dinner included a few Italian specialties, including ricotta manicotti and fried polenta (cornmeal) in the chef's own marinara sauce.[11]

Celebrity Meets
★ Royalty

De Laurentiis was more than happy to volunteer her cooking services for a charity event in Santa Barbara, California, in 2011. That she got to serve lunch to Prince William and his wife Kate, the Duchess of Cambridge, just happened to be a lucky bonus.

De Laurentiis told *People* magazine that meeting the prince flustered her a bit. "I don't even remember what came out of my mouth," she recalled of the moment she placed a plate of her sweet-corn lasagna in front of him. "And I put my hand on his shoulder after I was told not to have any contact. At that point I ran away."[12]

The polo match was held by a group of American supporters of the foundation started by the royal couple and the duke's brother, Prince Harry. The Royal Foundation helps children and veterans and encourages sustainable development.

More recently, De Laurentiis was in charge of food preparation for the 2015 edition of Keep Memory Alive's annual Power of Love fund-raiser for the Cleveland Clinic Lou Ruvo Center for Brain Health. The center conducts research into Alzheimer's, Huntington's, and Parkinson's diseases, which are associated with brain and memory disorders. De Laurentiis was the head chef in the gala's kitchen, leading a team of chefs organized by her former Spago employer, Wolfgang Puck.[13]

De Laurentiis also has helped charitable causes using more of her natural gifts—her looks. In 2014, Giada participated in the Heart Truth Dress Collection fashion show in New York City. Go Red For Women benefits the American Heart Association and is a campaign in which wearing red helps raise aware-ness for women's risk of heart attack and stroke. De Laurentiis joined several other celebrities in walking the runway wearing designer red gowns.

The woman who once was accused of being a model instead of a chef said she came away from the event with a whole new appreciation for those who work fashion shows. "I used to think being a model and walking the runway was an easy job, but I have changed my mind. I have so much respect for those women because it's a tough job!"[14]

Taste of the City

For years De Laurentiis has made appearances at various food festivals, which typically benefit a worthy cause or two. She is a regular at the New York City Wine & Food Festival, sponsored by the organization that launched her into celebrity chefdom, *Food & Wine* magazine. The 2015 edition of the event benefited Food Bank for New York City and anti-hunger nonprofit Share Our Strength's "No Kid Hungry" program. That year, Giada De

Parmegiano-reggiano cheese is a classic Italian ingredient and one that Giada frequently uses in her recipes. She thinks it is important to use the freshest, most authentic ingredients you can find in your dishes.

Giada often attends the New York City Food & Wine Festival, where she meets fans, brings awareness to her causes, and of course, tastes food and wine!

Laurentiis's Italian Feast kicked off the festival's slate of more than one hundred individual tasting events. The theme of the feast was an Italian Sunday supper with the family—something the event's host knew from personal experience.

In previous years, De Laurentiis presided over a meatball-making contest known as Meatball Madness. Restaurant chefs from New York City competed to make the best meatballs. The overall winner was chosen by a panel of professional chefs, while attendee tasters had control over who received the People's Choice award.

Although De Laurentiis usually did not act as a judge at these events, she did get to taste many of the competitors' entries while trying to keep the madness under control as host. There may not be a tastier way for a celebrity chef to support a worthy cause.

Chapter 6

Recipe for
Becoming a Chef

Chefs are like snowflakes, in that no two are exactly alike. Yet there are several similar key moves someone can make in order to become a professional cook. The path that Giada De Laurentiis took to make it in this career field can be a good one to follow. Her passion for food, a desire to get the best training available to her, and experience in several different types of professional cooking make her an excellent example of how to pursue this career field successfully.

Craving a Career

It's never too early to begin thinking about what one wants to do in life. After all, De Laurentiis started cooking at a very young age, making pizza dough by the time she was five years old. That was because she had a strong interest in the creation of delicious food, even as a child. Although she really got interested in being a chef in her teens, she claims to have known early on that she wanted to have a job that involved food in some way.

One of the first indications that someone is destined to be a chef is being passionate about food and all things food related. People who care deeply about food, who are known as "foodies," make the best cooks and chefs. Foodies are not just those who simply like eating or enjoy going out to restaurants. They live and breathe food. They talk about recipes and cooking a lot, rate the menus and dishes at every eatery they visit, read articles about food trends, join cooking clubs or classes, and watch shows like De Laurentiis's with great regularity.

Not everyone who wants to be a chef has to be a total foodie. However, a deep and lasting interest in planning, preparing, cooking, and sharing meals is a very good place to start.

Teach Your Children Well

De Laurentiis was surrounded by amateur chefs in her extended family. A passion for food ran through several generations. Her grandfather, mother, and aunt did not just share their joy of cooking around the dinner table. They made sure that young Giada was right there beside them in the kitchen, at home, and at Dino De Laurentiis's Italian food shop.

Many aspiring chefs grew up as De Laurentiis did, learning how to cook from watching and helping their mothers or fathers create family meals. They did not, however, have access to a professional shop or restaurant as she did. While it is not necessary for prospective chefs to follow her path exactly, it is important that they have someone available and willing to show them the ropes. Young chef hopefuls certainly need someone to show them how to cook. Training can come from parents, other family members, or even a friendly neighbor who is willing to take the time and make the effort.

Culinary training can be achieved in many ways. Taking a cooking class through your school is one way for aspiring chefs to learn food preparation.

Another possibility is that kids might learn how to cook in school. Back in the 1950s and '60s, schools regularly offered a class called "home economics." Everything a person needed to know about running a household was covered, including how to shop for food and cook. Over the years, things changed. Schools, particularly high schools, began to focus more on teaching children how to get a job than the basic life skills found in home ec classes. Some saw the value in teaching life skills and continued to offer classes in this specific area. Unfortunately, many of those schools have had to downplay or eliminate courses covering life skills such as cooking because of budget concerns.

""There are a lot of kids out there who have talents, but we wait too long to expose them," she once told a reporter for *Redbook* magazine, talking about the kinds of life skills taught in school.[1]

The good news is that students who would like to become professional chefs do not have to rely on their schools to teach them the culinary arts. Community education programs frequently offer cooking or food and wine classes. These courses, sponsored by local governments or private organizations, can be as simple as a one-night lesson in how to make a particular dish. Or they may go more in depth, spending several weeks covering a specific type of cuisine or using food that can be found during a particular season or region of the world. Cooking schools have been known to open their kitchen doors to children and teenagers for age-appropriate cooking lessons.

More Than One Path to Learning

When she finished high school, De Laurentiis was persuaded to go to college and study something other than cooking and food preparation. Believe it or not, this was not necessarily a bad thing for an aspiring chef. While a degree in social anthropology may not have helped De Laurentiis in her career as a chef, there are college-level courses that can be useful to someone looking to make cooking their life's work. Many colleges and universities offer classes in hospitality, a field that includes cooking and food service. Even someone who is studying a totally different field can take hospitality classes as electives, which are courses that are not required by a college to graduate with a particular degree. Students may also be able to minor in hospitality or get a double degree.

Culinary school is an intense and rigorous path to becoming a chef. If you decide to take this route, be prepared to work hard. But also be prepared to learn a lot!

Having an associate or bachelor's degree in business or marketing would be beneficial for anyone who wanted to start their own cooking business, as De Laurentiis did when she started GDL Foods. Getting a college degree is a good idea as a fallback, in case a cooking career does not pan out or the aspiring chef changes his or her mind somewhere down the road.

Aside from getting a college degree, someone hoping to become a chef or professional cook would be smart to attend some kind of cooking school. Enrolling in Le Cordon Bleu—in Paris or on any one of the branch campuses—is not necessary.

On-the-Job
★ Experience

Having a college degree usually proves helpful when applying for culinary school or a job cooking in a restaurant kitchen. However, working somewhere as a cook or a chef also can open a lot of doors in the culinary world. Almost every culinary school worth its salt offers students the chance to perform an internship. Interns work in the food service industry while taking classes, and they learn by doing. Typically schools arrange to place students with restaurants and other organizations. Instead of pay, most interns simply receive credit toward their degrees.

There are plenty of culinary arts schools that may not have the name recognition of that famous institution, but they will give students a thorough understanding of cooking practices and hands-on experience.

Students graduate from the majority of culinary arts schools with an associate or bachelor's degree. Most offer the chance to study general cuisine or specialties such as baking and pastries. Those who are ambitious, as De Laurentiis was, can look into studying both areas. Another option is to pursue certification as a chef, rather than a degree. To become certified, prospective chefs have to take courses and pass a written exam.

The Restaurant Route

Once someone has received training as a chef, it is time to land a job. Many new chefs have an eye toward getting a position in a restaurant, mainly because this is traditionally where the majority of jobs in this field can be found. It is important to remember that almost no one walks into a restaurant as a new chef and gets a head cook position. There are several levels one has to work their way through to get to the top of the kitchen food chain.

Beginning chefs, even some who have had culinary school or other training, usually start by assisting others. After putting in time in this position, learning from other chefs on the job, they may get promoted to being a line cook, working as a chef at a specific station. This is the job that De Laurentiis performed at Spago, when she worked the pastry station.

If she had decided to continue working as a restaurant chef, she might have moved on to being an executive chef. Of course, once she opened her own restaurant, she performed many of the duties of an executive chef—menu planning, hiring, etc.

Other Avenues

De Laurentiis worked in restaurant kitchens at the start of her career. But then she decided to go in a different direction and try other food- and cooking-related paths. These included personal chef and caterer.

Becoming a personal chef is an option for someone with a background in food and nutrition. Personal or private chefs operate their own businesses. Some work in the kitchens of their clients, as De Laurentiis often did. Others might prepare meals in their own kitchens and bring the food to the client's home for storage and use over a period of time. Still others might find

Types of Chefs

In fine restaurants, beginning chefs are referred to as commis chefs. These chefs-in-training do a little bit of everything, learning to work at each of several stations found in a professional kitchen.

The next step up is station chef. Kitchen stations generally include meat, vegetable, fish, and pastry. Often there is even a station specifically for sauces.

Station chefs may get a promotion to sous chef. Considered the second-in-command, a sous chef is basically an assistant manager of the kitchen.

Head or executive chefs run the kitchen. Duties include ordering ingredients, managing staff, budgeting, and other administrative tasks in addition to creating menus and recipes, and, of course, actually cooking.

themselves cooking in an industrial or corporate kitchen when working for a business executive.

Caterers operate similarly to personal chefs. In addition to doing cooking and serving meals, caterers may also be responsible for other parts of event planning and preparation. This can include renting a location and decorating it. Unlike personal chefs, who basically operate on their own, caterers often have to hire staff to help serve the meal. In most states

A love of food and a talent for making it can lead to many different careers.

caterers must get a license to run their business, just as restaurants that serve the general public must do.

Both personal chefs and caterers plan menus, do the shopping for food and other ingredients, and, in the case of caterers, set up the dining area. One of the less glamorous jobs done by both involves cleaning up after the cooking. Caterers also have to clear event locations of any materials used in the course of their jobs, in both the kitchen and the dining area.

Advice From Giada

Over the years, De Laurentiis has been asked, by interviewers and home cooks alike, what advice she would give to someone who wants to cook. Her replies have ranged from the practical, with regard to training and what tools to have on hand, to the philosophical, concerning the type of mind-set someone should have to make it in the culinary field.

Regarding kitchen tools, De Laurentiis recommends that home cooks invest in at least two professional-grade knives, one for slicing and chopping and one for paring. Each should be easy to handle and feel good when they are held—not too heavy, not too bulky. Other absolute necessities, in her opinion, are nonstick pans, a pasta pot, and a pasta scooper. She also highly recommends a microplane or grater, "to zest everything under the sun."[2] As she said in an interview, "If you have tools you enjoy using you'll probably get in the kitchen a lot more."[3]

First and foremost, for those who want to become professional chefs, she has stressed the importance of learning by doing. Taking classes is one way to accomplish this. Gaining experience also can be anything from a school internship to volunteering as a chef for a family or neighborhood gathering. According to De Laurentiis, "Being involved, learning firsthand and observing the craft and absorbing all you can, makes it easier to define what you want. It will also ultimately make you a better chef."[4]

"I didn't plan on having this career, I just rode the wave. And now I'm contemplating where it leads."

And what has she herself learned from years of being a chef? Being in the kitchen has taught her many life lessons, including not to sweat the small stuff as much.

"Cooking teaches you to improvise," she said in an interview, "and that's important in life. I think I have learned to go

Even after spending all day cooking and working with food, Giada is still excited to come home and cook for her family.

Giada still uses many of the skills she learned as a caterer and a food stylist. Here, she hosts a brunch for the Food Network & Cooking Channel's South Beach Wine & Food Festival in 2015.

with the flow more now, and I don't have to be so regimented or controlling. If a new recipe doesn't work out exactly how I wrote it, I am more relaxed about it."[5]

In the end, being a professional chef comes down to four main ingredients: "skill, determination, perseverance, and hard work ... If you can do all of that, then you can be successful."[6]

Chapter
7

Awards, Achievements, and Endorsements

As just about everyone can attest, it is nice to be acknowledged and appreciated. Giada De Laurentiis, like every chef, must feel greatly rewarded by seeing how guests enjoy the meals she prepares. However, she also enjoys the awards she has been given by the television and culinary industries. While De Laurentiis's cookbooks have wound up on the *New York Times* Best Seller List, it is her television shows that have brought home the serious hardware, in the form of several Daytime Emmy Awards. Additionally, De Laurentiis worked her way to a spot in the Culinary Hall of Fame.

Her status as a celebrity chef also has earned De Laurentiis several endorsement deals. An endorsement is when the image or words of someone famous are used to help sell a product or service. In other words, a celebrity gets paid for giving his or her support, or seal of approval. De Laurentiis has been talented and fortunate enough to take advantage of several such deals.

Giada no longer works behind the scene at awards ceremonies. Now she's invited as a nominee and winner.

An Emmy Rundown

For years, the Daytime Emmy Awards have featured a number of categories in which De Laurentiis and her shows have been nominated. These include awards for directing and technical work such as editing. The flashier, or more popular, categories are Outstanding Culinary Program and Outstanding Culinary Host. (Until 2013 the culinary category was combined with "lifestyle" programs and hosts.) Each year from 2006 through 2015, either De Laurentiis herself, her shows, or members of her crew—sometimes all three—have been nominated for a Daytime Emmy.

> *Jade, looking at Giada's Emmy shelf: "Mom, the angels up there … I think they need to be cleaned."*

De Laurentiis has brought home one Daytime Emmy Awards for hosting, for *Everyday Italian* in 2008. That was the year that the show swept all of the awards for which it was nominated: best host, best directing (Juliette D'Annible), and best show. Two years before, *Everyday Italian* had won its first Emmy Award, for directing (Irene Wong).

Giada at Home has been nominated in one category or another since it first aired in 2008 through the eighth season in 2015. De Laurentiis herself has been nominated for outstanding host four times for her duties on this program, but as of 2015, she had not yet won. The show itself won another Outstanding Lifestyle/Culinary Emmy in 2010.

Best directing honors went to Anne Fox, who also happens to be De Laurentiis's business partner in Linguine Pictures, three years in a row (2009–2011) for her work on *Giada at*

Home. Fox won an additional directing Emmy in 2014 for *Giada in Paradise.* The series began life on the Food Network back in 2007. New episodes were taped and aired on sister network, the Cooking Channel, beginning in 2013. It was for the series reboot on the Cooking Channel that Fox was honored as a director.

Additional Honors

The National Academy of Television Arts and Sciences, which presents the Daytime Emmys, is not the only organization to commend De Laurentiis for her work in television. Since 1975, the Alliance for Women in Media has presented the Gracie Awards. These awards are given to those responsible for delivering quality programming created by, for, and about women. The alliance wishes to honor television, radio, and web programming that shows women in a realistic light, as strong, complex individuals. De Laurentiis was the recipient of the 2012 Gracie Award for Outstanding Host—Lifestyle.

Good food not only helps people stay healthy but can also be a great comfort to those who are sick. People with HIV/AIDS, cancer, or other serious illnesses in Los Angeles County can get free, nutritious meals delivered to them by an agency that operates under the name Project Angel Food. In 2013, De Laurentiis was the inaugural recipient of the organization's Iconic Chef Award. She was honored "for her leadership in helping people connect delicious food with nutritious eating and a healthy lifestyle."[1]

De Laurentiis said she was honored to receive the award and expressed her appreciation for Project Angel Food: "The work they do providing meals to thousands in need is something I've long admired."[2]

Pasta and Pyrex

One of the perks of being a celebrity chef is receiving offers to promote food- and cooking-related products or even to create your own line of culinary goods. De Laurentiis's first national endorsement deal was with the pasta manufacturer Barilla in 2006. She signed on as a spokesperson for the brand in the United States, and her image appeared in a series of advertisements that appeared in print publications. Two years later, De Laurentiis signed a deal with Academia Barilla, the Italian arm of the company, to produce a small line of specialty Italian food products under the name Giada De Laurentiis Selected. Items included olive oil, balsamic vinegar, sea salt with lemon zest, and a prepackaged Tuscan Herb Mix. The products were available through the Crate and Barrel chain of home-goods stores.

"My relationship with Academia Barilla is an obvious one, combining my love for traditional Italian cooking with the best ingredients available," said De Laurentiis.[3]

In between the two deals with Barilla, in 2007, De Laurentiis signed an endorsement deal with the cookware manufacturer Pyrex. According to a press release at the time, it was the company's first such deal with a celebrity.[4] The marketing campaign required the celebrity chef to appear in commercials for Pyrex products, as well as a sweepstakes, with dinner cooked by De Laurentiis in the winner's home as the prize. A selection of her recipes was included in the purchase of certain items as well.

The pairing of De Laurentiis and Pyrex was made at the suggestion of marketing firm Two/Ten, based in Chicago. Research indicated that Pyrex was a trusted brand, but it was considered a bit "old-fashioned." Having De Laurentiis endorse the company's new Accents Collection cooking and bakeware was a move designed to appeal to young, beginning cooks who

Like many celebrity chefs, Giada endorses some of her favorite products, including Barilla pasta.

were more likely to be familiar with the chef's work on the Food Network. The marketing campaign with De Laurentiis worked so well that Pyrex renewed her contract for an additional year.[5]

On Target

De Laurentiis kicked off 2010 in fine fashion, announcing that she had signed a deal with Target to feature a line of kitchen products bearing her name. The cookware, baking dishes, and small appliances in the Giada De Laurentiis for Target collection took their cue from their namesake chef. They were designed for everyday use by home cooks, much like De Laurentiis's recipes. Specialty foods, such as pasta sauces and flavored coffees, were also part of the specialty line.

Target stores had started selling groceries a few years before, and those departments were doing well. Adding De Laurentiis-branded items was seen as a move to strengthen sales even further. As a Target grocery spokesperson, she also gave cooking demonstrations and signed her cookbooks at some stores.[6]

At first, the Giada De Laurentiis for Target line was available only in US stores. The products were introduced in Canadian stores in 2013.[7] "Food Network Canada is a big part of my life," De Laurentiis said at a 2013 event for the Canadian media, "and now my stuff at Target can be a big part of everybody's life. I'm very excited that I've been able to be a partner for three years, and I'm even more excited that now it's available to everybody in Canada."[8]

The Face of "Beautiful Night"

The same year that De Laurentiis signed with Target in the United States, she also agreed to partner with wine maker Bella

Tops in
★ Sauce

Her television programs are not the only De Laurentiis-branded items that have received special recognition. In 2011, *Consumer Reports* named De Laurentiis's Tomato Basil red sauce, part of the Target line of products, a "best buy" in its review of twelve celebrity pasta sauces. Her product beat out other celebrity sauces by the likes of fellow celebrity chef Mario Batali and popular favorite Paul Newman.[9]

In 2012, the magazine ranked some twenty sauces, celebrity branded and otherwise. The judging was based not only on taste but also on nutrition, overall cost, and value per serving. Again De Laurentiis's product emerged victorious, edging out Batali's, which came in second. Her product also topped a number of non-celebrity-branded commercial sauces, including that of her former sponsor, Barilla.[10]

Giada's line of gourmet food products are extremely popular.

Sera. There were a few natural connections between the chef and the wines she was endorsing. For one thing, both originated in Italy. Also, food and wine go together quite well. That, in fact, is why Bella Sera chose to partner with De Laurentiis. Her first job was to create recipes to be specifically paired with the company's wines.

At the time, De Laurentiis commented, "I believe that delicious food deserves delicious wine, so Bella Sera and I have partnered to create food and wine pairings that bring a taste of Italy to home."[11]

Within a year of signing the contract starting their endorsement deal, the two parties joined forces on the "Beautiful

Evenings with Bella Sera" contest. Members of De Laurentiis's fan base, meaning home cooks, were called upon to send in recipes they made up themselves. Additionally, contestants needed to come up with a movie and bottle of Bella Sera wine that would go perfectly with their recipe. De Laurentiis would help company executives judge which entry was the winner. The idea behind the contest was suggested by the company's name: Bella Sera means "beautiful night" in Italian.

"A beautiful evening can be as simple as watching a favorite movie while enjoying an excellent meal and delicious wine at home," De Laurentiis was quoted as saying in a press release regarding the contest. "This is why I've partnered with Bella Sera on this fun recipe contest."[12]

The Colorful Chef

In 2012, De Laurentiis signed an endorsement deal that had more to do with her looks than with her cooking. The hair-care company Clairol signed her to be a celebrity spokesperson for its Natural Instincts brand of hair color. "I've been wanting this for a long time," she said of being hired to promote a beauty product.[13]

De Laurentiis was excited to partner with Clairol because she felt the brand represented freedom of expression. In this way, women could achieve a kind of inner beauty that matched how the company's products made them look on the outside. Speaking about Clairol, she said, "They build confidence in a woman and what she does with her hair. I do it through the kitchen—and now through beauty as well."[14]

She noted that she used to simply let her hair get natural highlights from being out in the sun. However, when she lost

A Sad
☆ Farewell

While her professional life was going full-steam ahead, De Laurentiis was encountering some difficulties at home. In December 2014, she and Thompson announced that they were getting divorced. The couple had been together for twenty-six years, married for eleven of those. "That's a lifetime with someone," De Laurentiis told a reporter in November 2015.

"It was a very difficult time," she recalled in the same interview. "I don't have the answers. I'm figuring them out as I go."

One bright spot of this sad news was that De Laurentiis learned that she could take care of herself: "Every challenge is an opportunity to become stronger and believe in yourself more."[15]

her brother to skin cancer, she decided to stay out of the sun and to get a color boost to her hair by cosmetic means.

Giada Going Forward

With the premiere of the six-part Food Network series *Giada Entertains* in January 2016, De Laurentiis began another commercial partnership. Online home-furnishings and house-wares company Wayfair Inc. offered viewers the chance to buy merchandise featured in, or inspired by, items seen during each episode.[16]

So what lies ahead for celebrity chef Giada De Laurentiis? She mentioned to an interviewer that she would like to work more with children in public schools, presumably continuing her volunteer work planting gardens, but also helping students in the classroom. She would like to be part of a movement that brings life skills classes back full force. "Schools are supposed to prepare kids for the real world," she said, "and I feel like we need that again."[17]

It is also a safe bet that De Laurentiis will continue hosting television cooking shows, writing best-selling cookbooks, and overseeing operations at her Las Vegas restaurant. But even if the celebrity aspect of being a chef were to disappear tomorrow, chances are that she would still be cooking, no matter what and no matter where.

"I know why I fell in love with cooking; because it makes me happy. And because it's the place that I feel the strongest, the most empowered, the most creative," De Laurentiis said. "It's where I can stand on my own two feet and know who I am, truly."[18]

Try It Yourself!

Pan-Roasted Fish with Candied Lemon and Dijon

Serves: 4

Ingredients

¼ c (50 g) white sugar

2 tablespoons (30 mL) water

2 lemons, peeled and segmented

1 teaspoon (5 mL) Dijon mustard

2 tbsp (30 mL) olive oil

1 tbsp (15 mL) chopped fresh basil

salt and pepper, to taste

4 6-oz (150 g) swordfish or tuna steaks

arugula and tomatoes, for salad

Directions

1.) In a small saucepan, combine sugar and water. Bring to a boil, stirring so the sugar will dissolve.

2.) Add lemon segments and simmer 2–3 minutes, until the lemon is fragrant. Turn off heat and allow liquid to cool.

3.) Remove the segments and set aside.

4.) In a small bowl, whisk together 2 tbsp of the liquid with the Dijon mustard and 2 tbsp olive oil. Add salt and pepper to taste.

5.) Heat a skillet over medium-high heat.

6.) Season the fish with salt, pepper, and olive oil.

7.) Carefully place the fish in the preheated skillet.

8.) Cook on each side about 3–4 minutes (for medium), depending on the thickness of the steaks. They should be browned in color but still slightly soft in the center.

9.) In a large bowl, combine arugula, tomatoes, and any other vegetables you'd like (cucumber, olives, marinated artichokes, even roasted peppers) with half of the candied lemon and Dijon dressing. Toss gently, so as not to bruise the arugula.

10.) Serve the fish with the salad, topping with remaining dressing. Use the lemon segments for garnish.

Braised Beef Short Ribs

Serves: 4

Ingredients

4–5 lbs (2200 g) beef short ribs, bone-in

4 tbsp (60 mL) olive oil

1 tbsp (15 mL) red wine vinegar

2 sprigs rosemary

1 portobello mushroom, cleaned and sliced

3 cloves garlic, minced

2 tbsp (30 mL) flour

1 tsp (5 mL) paprika

2 cups (475 mL) chicken, beef, or
    vegetable stock

salt and pepper to taste

Directions

1.) Combine salt, pepper, paprika, and flour in a large bowl.

2.) Toss the short ribs in flour mixture until all the meat is lightly coated.

3.) Preheat a large skillet with a lid over medium-high heat. When the pan is hot, add about half the olive oil.

4.) Place the floured short ribs over the heat. Brown (about 2–3 minutes) on each side.

5.) Add the vinegar, garlic, rosemary, stock, and remaining olive oil. Add more salt and pepper, if desired.

6.) Cover and reduce heat to low.

7.) Simmer until the meat can be pulled from the bone with a fork (1½ to 2 hours).

8.) Add mushrooms and cook for an additional 5 minutes, or until they are soft.

9.) Serve short ribs with roasted vegetables, spooning the liquid and mushrooms on top.

Lemon Spaghetti

Serves: 4

Ingredients

1 lb (454 g) package spaghetti

2 lemons (yielding 1 tbsp lemon zest and about ½ c juice)

2/3 c (160 mL) grated Parmesan cheese

2/3 c (160 mL) olive oil

1 clove garlic, minced

1/3 c (80 mL) chopped fresh basil

salt and pepper to taste

Directions

1.) Prepare spaghetti according to package instructions.

2.) In a large saucepan, sauté the garlic in a bit of the olive oil until it becomes fragrant (about 2 minutes over medium heat).

3.) Add the remaining olive oil, salt, pepper, lemon juice and zest. Cook for about 2 minutes, or until thoroughly warmed.

4.) Drain spaghetti and place in the pan with olive oil and lemon juice mixture.

5.) Add the cheese and basil, and then carefully toss all ingredients together. Garnish with additional basil, cheese, or crushed pepper if desired.

Balsamic Roasted Asparagus

Serves: 4

Ingredients

8 oz (227 g) asparagus, cleaned and ends
　removed

4 tbsp (60 mL) olive oil

2 tbsp (30 mL) balsamic vinegar

1 tsp (5 mL) paprika

salt

pepper

½ tsp (2.5 mL) crushed red pepper

1 tbsp (15 mL) Italian herb blend (dried
　oregano, basil, parsley, and rosemary)

pinch of sugar

Directions

1.) Preheat oven to 350° F (176° C).

2.) In a quart-sized Ziploc bag, combine all ingredients.

3.) Close the bag tightly and shake until asparagus is covered in all the spices, vinegar, and oil.

4.) Spread on a baking sheet and bake for about 10–15 minutes, or until asparagus is tender.

Pomodoro Sauce

Serves: 4–6

Ingredients

1 32-oz (1 L) can of crushed tomatoes

4 cloves of garlic

1 large handful basil, chopped

1 tsp salt

1 tsp pepper

3 tbsp olive oil

Directions

1.) In a large bowl, combine all ingredients.

2.) Let rest and macerate (let the juices pool) for at least 2 hours. Or you can jar this and keep it in the refrigerator/pantry for as long as you'd like.

3.) Remove garlic before serving.

4.) Use on pizza, pastas, parmigiana, meatballs, or anything else that needs a simple, light tomato sauce. Add capers and olives for a puttanesca, or cooked sausage and crushed red pepper for a spicy diavolo sauce.

Eggplant Parmigiana

Serves: 4

Ingredients

2 large eggplants, sliced into ½ inch (13 mm) rounds

1 c (90 g) parmesan cheese, grated

½ c (30 g) mozzarella cheese

1 c (90 g) ricotta

½ c (30 g) fontina cheese, grated

2 cups (180 g) pomodoro sauce, plus extra for serving

handful fresh basil, chopped

olive oil

salt and pepper to taste

Directions

1.) Grease a large casserole dish with olive oil.

2.) Preheat oven to 350° F (176° C).

3.) Generously season eggplant slices with salt, pepper, and olive oil.

4.) Using a large spoon, pour a bit of the pomodoro sauce on the bottom of the casserole dish, creating a thin layer.

5.) Place a few of the slices of eggplant in a single layer on top of the pomodoro sauce in the baking dish.

6.) Add another layer of pomodoro sauce.

7.) Add a thin layer of ricotta, then mozzarella, Parmesan, and fontina.

8.) Add another layer of the eggplant, then sauce, and then cheese until all ingredients are used. Make sure the final (top) layer is extra cheesy.

9.) Bake in oven for about 20–30 minutes, or until eggplant is softened and all the cheese is melted.

10.) Garnish with fresh basil and crushed red pepper, if desired.

Baked Pasta with Béchamel

Serves: 4–6

Ingredients

1 stick (60 mL) butter

½ c (60 g) plus 2 tbsp flour

1 quart (1 L) whole milk

1 cup (90 g) grated fontina

½ lb (230 g) pancetta or prosciutto, diced

salt and pepper to taste

1 lb (454 g) dry rigatoni, penne, or fusilli

3 tbsp (45 g) butter, diced

Directions

1.) Cook pasta according to package instructions.

2.) Preheat oven to 425° F (218° C).

3.) Grease a 9x13 in (23x33 cm) baking dish.

4.) In a large saucepan, melt stick of butter.

5.) Add flour and whisk until smooth (about 2 minutes).

6.) Whisk in milk slowly until smooth.

7.) Simmer until the sauce becomes thick enough to coat the back of a spoon (about 9 minutes).

8.) Remove from heat and stir in pancetta, nutmeg, and salt and pepper to taste.

9.) Drain the pasta and carefully pour it in the prepared baking dish.

10.) Using a wooden spoon, stir the béchamel sauce over top, making sure to coat every piece of pasta.

11.) Dot with the cubed butter and top with fontina cheese.

12.) Bake for 25 minutes, or until the sauce is bubbling and the cheese has created a golden crust.

Minestrone Soup

Serves: 4–6

Ingredients

1 12-oz (350 mL) can red kidney beans

1 12-oz (350 mL) can diced tomatoes

3 c (710 mL) chicken or vegetable stock

3 large carrots, sliced

½ cup (120 mL) green beans, chopped (frozen or fresh)

3 celery stalks, chopped

1 medium-sized onion, diced

3 cloves of garlic

1 cup (140 g) dried pasta such as macaroni, diteli, canneroni, gemelli, or any other small shapes

1 handful rosemary

1 handful thyme

1 handful oregano

½ tsp crushed red pepper

salt and pepper, to taste

1 tbsp (15 mL) olive oil

Directions

1.) Using a piece of cooking twine, tie the herbs together.

2.) In a large soup pot, heat up olive oil and add the carrots, celery, onion, and garlic. Cook for five minutes, or until the vegetables become fragrant.

3.) Add stock, herbs, spices, kidney beans, and tomatoes. Simmer, covered, for 1 hour.

4.) Make sure the liquid is boiling (turn up the heat if you need to). Add the pasta and the green beans. Boil for 7–10 minutes, or until pasta is cooked al dente. Remove the bundle of herbs.

5.) Serve with crusty bread and a drizzle of olive oil.

Simple Chocolate and Cinnamon Fudge

Serves: 4–6

Ingredients

3 tbsp (45 g) butter at room temperature, plus more for greasing a pan

1 14-oz (414 mL) can of sweetened condensed milk

2 tsp (10 mL) ground cinnamon

1 tsp (5 mL) vanilla extract

2 c (150 mL) bittersweet chocolate chips/chunks

sea salt

Directions

1.) Grease the bottom and sides of an 8x8 in (20x20 cm) baking pan. Line the pan with a sheet of parchment paper large enough to go over the sides of the pan. This will make it easier to pull out the fudge when it's finished.

2.) Dice the butter into squares. Make sure it's room temperature: this will make the dicing easier and ensure that it combines easily with the other ingredients.

3.) In a medium-sized stainless steel or glass bowl, combine condensed milk, cinnamon, and vanilla.

4.) Place the bowl over a pot with about 1 in (2.5 cm) of boiling water. The steam created by this will melt the chocolate and butter slowly and consistently.

5.) Add butter and chocolate, stirring constantly. Be sure to use an oven mitt to hold on to the bowl, as it will get very hot as the ingredients incorporate.

6.) When mixture is fully melted and combined (about 6 minutes), pour mixture into prepared pan. Be sure to use a rubber spatula to make sure you get all of the batter!

7.) Sprinkle the top with sea salt (if desired).

8.) Refrigerate for at least 2 hours, or until firm.

9.) Run a knife under hot water, then slide around the edge of the pan to loosen the fudge. Pull out with the parchment paper edges. Peel off paper, and cut fudge into 1in (2.5 cm) pieces.

Orange Ricotta Pound Cake

Serves: 6–8

Ingredients

1½ c flour

2½ tsp baking powder

1 tsp fine salt

¾ c (1½ sticks) butter, softened; plus a
little more to grease the pan

1½ cups whole milk ricotta cheese

1½ cups white sugar, plus 1 tbsp

3 large eggs

1 tsp (5 mL) vanilla extract

zest of one orange

1 tbsp (5 mL) almond extract

3 oranges, peeled and cut into supremes

powdered sugar for dusting

Directions

1.) Preheat oven to 350° F (176° C).

2.) Grease all sides and bottom of a 9x5x3 in (23x13x8 cm) loaf pan with butter.

3.) In a medium-sized mixing bowl, sift the flour, baking soda, and salt.

4.) Cream together the butter, ricotta, and sugar using an electric mixer. In about 3 minutes (on high speed), the mixture should be fluffy and light in color.

5.) Add eggs, one at a time, mixing between each addition.

6.) Add the vanilla, almond extract, and orange zest, mixing until well combined.

7.) Add dry ingredients, a little at a time, until fully mixed.

8.) Pour mixture into prepared pan. Be sure to use a rubber spatula to get out all of the batter.

9.) Bake about 45–50 minutes, or until a toothpick comes out clean and the cake is starting to pull away from the sides of the pan.

10.) While cake is baking, place the oranges in a small bowl, along with 1 tbsp sugar, a splash of vanilla, and a sprinkle of ground cinnamon. Allow this to macerate, or let the juices pool from the oranges.

11.) To serve, slice the cake and serve with a spoonful of the oranges and their juice and dust with powdered sugar.

SELECTED RESOURCES BY GIADA De LAURENTIIS

Television Series and Specials

Everyday Italian

Behind the Bash

Giada's Weekend Getaways

Food Network Star

Giada at Home

Giada in Italy

Giada Entertains

Cookbooks

Everyday Italian: 125 Simple and Delicious Recipes (2005)

Giada's Family Dinners (2006)

Everyday Pasta (2007)

Giada's Kitchen: New Italian Favorites (2008)

Giada at Home: Family Recipes from Italy and California (2010)

Weeknights with Giada: Quick and Simple Recipes to Revamp Dinner (2012)

Giada's Feel Good Food: My Healthy Recipes and Secrets (2013)

Happy Cooking: Make Every Meal Count . . . Without Stressing Out (2015)

Restaurant

Giada

CHRONOLOGY

★

1970—Born on August 22, 1970

1978—Moves with mother and siblings to the United States

1996—Graduates from UCLA

1997—Graduates from Le Cordon Bleu

2002—Is discovered by Food Network executives through a piece in *Food & Wine* magazine

2003—*Everyday Italian* premieres on the Food Network

2003—Marries longtime boyfriend Todd Thompson

2003—Loses her brother Dino to melanoma

2005—*Everyday Italian* cookbook is published

2006—*Behind the Bash* premieres

2006—*Giada's Family Dinners* hits store shelves

2007—*Giada's Weekend Getaway* debuts

2007—Appears for the first time as a guest judge on *The Next Food Network Star*

2007—*Everyday Pasta* cookbook published

2008—Daughter Jade is born

2008—Wins Daytime Emmy for Outstanding Lifestyle Host

2008—Publishes *Giada's Kitchen*

2009—Voice actor on *Handy Manny*

2010—Begins endorsement relationship with Target

2010—*Giada at Home* published

2010—Her grandfather, movie producer Dino De Laurentiis, dies

2012—*Weeknights with Giada* published

2012—Wins Gracie Award and is inducted into the Culinary Hall of Fame

2013—*Giada's Feel Good Food* cookbook is published

2014—Opens first restaurant, Giada, on the Las Vegas strip

2014—Is featured as a voice actor on *Pixie Hollow Bake Off*

2014—Announces separation from her husband

2015—*Happy Cooking* hits stores

CHAPTER NOTES

Chapter 1: Film and Food

1. Monica Corcoran, "Giada's Summer Magic," *Redbook*, June 2009, p. 128.
2. Jancee Dunn, "Giada's recipe for the good life," *Redbook*, January 2008, p. 86+.
3. Corcoran, "Giada's Summer Magic."
4. Jocelyn McClurg, "Giada De Laurentiis Serves a 'Recipe for Adventure,'" *USA Today*, August 29, 2013, p. 4D.
5. Liza Hamm, "Chatter: In the Kitchen with . . . Giada De Laurentiis," *People Weekly*, November 11, 2013, p. 112.
6. Julia Moskin, "Times Talks: Giada De Laurentiis and Giada De Laurentiis: Part 5," *New York Times*, October 13, 2012, http://www.nytimes.com/video/multimedia/100000002948607/flay-de-laurentiis-ddl-foodshow.html (accessed December 2015).
7. Ibid.
8. Lori Berger, "Giada Heats Things Up!" *Redbook*, February 2011, p. 130+.
9. Michelle Collins, "The Interview Where Giada De Laurentiis Stops Being Polite and Starts Getting Real," *Elle*, July 2014, http://www.elle.com/culture/news/a19407/food-network-giada-de-laurentiis-interview/ (accessed December 2015).
10. Shawna Malcolm, "Giada De Laurentiis Bets Big on Her First Restaurant, in Las Vegas: 'I Don't Do Anything Small,'" *Parade*, July 2014, http://parade.com/311389/shawnamalcom/giada-de-laurentiis-new-restaurant-las-vegas/ (accessed December 2015).
11. Berger, p. 128.
12. Moskin, "Times Talks: Giada De Laurentiis and Giada De Laurentiis: Part 4," *New York Times*, October 13, 2012, http://www.nytimes.com/video/multimedia/100000002948485/flay-de-laurentiis-shaming-my-family.html (accessed December 2015).
13. IMdB staff, "Biography: Giada De Laurentiis," IMdB.com, http://www.imdb.com/name/nm1373094/bio (accessed December 2015).

14. Berger, p. 130.
15. Corcoran, p. 128.

Chapter 2: Step by Step, Dish by Dish

1. Jeff Martin, narr., "Chefography: Giada De Laurentiis," The WorldNews (WN) Network, July 2015, http://wn.com/chefography (accessed December 2015).
2. Ibid.
3. Richard Ouzounian, "Giada De Laurentiis dishes on her delicious life: Big Interview," *The Toronto Star,* May 23, 2014, http://www .thestar.com/entertainment/television/2014/05/23/giada _de_laurentiis_dishes_on_her_delicious_life_big_interview.html (accessed January 2016).
4. Shawna Malcolm, "Giada De Laurentiis Bets Big on Her First Restaurant, in Las Vegas: 'I Don't Do Anything Small,'" *Parade,* July 2014, http://parade.com/311389/shawnamalcom/giada-de -laurentiis-new-restaurant-las-vegas/ (accessed December 2015).
5. Martin, narr., "Chefography: Giada De Laurentiis."
6. Staff, "Grand Diplôme, Paris," Le Cordon Bleu, https://www .cordonbleu.edu/paris/grand-diplome-cuisine-pastry/en (accessed January 2016).
7. Giada De Laurentiis, *Giada In Italy: Family Recipes From Italy and California* (New York: Clarkson Potter Publishers, 2010), p. 9.
8. Amazon.com staff, "Ciao, Bella! A Conversation with Giada De Laurentiis," Amazon, http://www.amazon.com/gp/feature .html?docId=557923 (accessed January 2016).
9. Monica Corcoran, "Giada's Summer Magic," *Redbook*, June 2009, p. 128.
10. Julia Moskin, "Times Talks: Giada De Laurentiis and Giada De Laurentiis: Part 2," *New York Times*, October 13, 2012, http:// www.nytimes.com/video/multimedia/100000002948481/flay-de -laurentiis-giadas-story.html (accessed December 2015).

11. Barbara Fairchild, "LA Times Festival of Books interview: Giada De Laurentiis," Cooking How.com YouTube channel, April 27, 2009, https://www.youtube.com/watch?v=pISVV1oIQAw (accessed December 2015).
12. Moskin, "Times Talks: Giada De Laurentiis and Giada De Laurentiis: Part 2."
13. Moskin, "Times Talk: Giada De Laurentiis and Giada De Laurentiis: Part 8," *New York Times*, October 13, 2012, http://www.nytimes.com/video/multimedia/100000002948751/flay-de-laurentiis-you-cant-teach-it.html (accessed December 2015).

Chapter 3: **Star of the Small Screen**

1. Julia Moskin, "Times Talks: Giada De Laurentiis and Giada De Laurentiis: Part 4," *New York Times*, October 13, 2012, http://www.nytimes.com/video/multimedia/100000002948485/flay-de-laurentiis-shaming-my-family.html (accessed December 2015).
2. Diana McKeon, "'Everything Italian' Fills Her House," *USA Today*, May 12, 2005, http://usatoday30.usatoday.com/life/lifestyle/2005-05-12-at-home_x.htm (accessed December 2015).
3. Editorial staff, "Giada De Laurentiis' Recipe for a Happy Life." *Shape*, http://www.shape.com/celebrities/giada-de-laurentiis-recipe-happy-life (accessed January 2016).
4. Moskin, "Times Talks: Giada De Laurentiis and Giada De Laurentiis: Part 4."
5. Shawna Malcolm, "Giada De Laurentiis Bets Big on Her First Restaurant, in Las Vegas: 'I Don't Do Anything Small,'" *Parade*, July 2014, http://parade.com/311389/shawnamalcom/giada-de-laurentiis-new-restaurant-las-vegas/ (accessed December 2015).
6. Jancee Dunn, "Giada's recipe for the good life," *Redbook*, January 2008, p. 86+.
7. Moskin, "Times Talks: Giada De Laurentiis and Giada De Laurentiis: Part 8," *New York Times*, October 13, 2012, http://www.nytimes.com/video/multimedia/100000002948751/flay-de-laurentiis-you-cant-teach-it.html (accessed December 2015).

8. Lori Berger, "Giada Heats Things Up!" *Redbook*, February 2011, p. 130+.

9. Sarika Dani, "New mom Giada: 'I've gained a partner in the kitchen,'" *Today.com*, June 27, 2008, http://www.today.com /id/25412222/ns/today-today_food/t/new-mom-giada-ive -gained-partner-kitchen/#.VofX8bYrJd (accessed January 2016).

10. Monica Corcoran, "Giada's summer magic," *Redbook*, June 2009, p. 128+.

11. Moskin, "Times Talks: Giada De Laurentiis and Giada De Laurentiis: Part 7," *New York Times*, October 13, 2012, http:// www.nytimes.com/video/multimedia/100000002948653/flay-de -laurentiis-not-the-best-cook.html (accessed December 2015).

12. Patricia Talorico, "Giada really hated losing to Rachael," the *Delaware News Journal*, August 11, 2014, http://www .delawareonline.com/story/secondhelpings/2014/08/11/giada -hated-losing-to-rachael/13899309/ (accessed December 2015).

13. Samantha Neudorf, "Giada De Laurentiis Stars in New TV Show," *The Daily Meal*, June 18, 2015, http://www.thedailymeal.com /news/eat/giada-de-laurentiis-stars-new-tv-show (accessed December 2015).

14. Cindy McLennan, "Giada Entertains: Food Network Series Debuts January 3," TV Series Finale, December 16, 2015, http:// tvseriesfinale.com/tv-show/giada-entertains-food-network -series-debuts-january-3/ (accessed December 2015).

15. Dunn, p. 86.

16. Alexia Elejalde-Ruiz, "Giada bonds with fans," Chicago Tribune, July 6, 2010, http://articles.chicagotribune .com/2010-07-06/features/ct-food-0707-giada-20100706_1 _food-network-cooking-italian-food (accessed December 2015).

17. Anna Monette Roberts, "The Story You Haven't Heard About Giada De Laurentiis' Rise to Fame," *Popsugar.com*, June 29, 2014, http://www.popsugar.com/food/Story-You-Havent-Heard -About-Giada-De-Laurentiis-Rise-Fame-35078008 (accessed January 2016).

Chapter 4: Books and Tables

1. Staff writer, "Nonfiction Review: Everyday Italian: 125 Simple and Delicious Recipes," Publishers Weekly, http://www.publishersweekly.com/978-1-4000-5258-5 (accessed January 2016).
2. Ibid.
3. David Kamp, "Kitchen Confidential," *Vanity Fair*, March 2006, p. 172.
4. Ibid.
5. Giada De Laurentiis, "Introduction," *Giada's Feel Good Food* (New York: Clarkson Potter Publishers, 2013), p. 9.
6. Staff, "FAQs," *Giada Weekly*, https://www.giadaweekly.com/faq (accessed January 2016).
7. Jocelyn McClurg, "Giada De Laurentiis serves a 'Recipe for Adventure,'" *USA Today*, August 29, 2013, p. 4D.
8. Staff, *Instructor*, Fall 2013, p. 9.
9. Julia Moskin, "Times Talks: Giada De Laurentiis and Giada De Laurentiis," *New York Times*, October 13, 2012.
10. Shawna Malcolm, "Giada De Laurentiis Bets Big on Her First Restaurant, in Las Vegas: 'I Don't Do Anything Small,'" *Parade*, July 2014, http://parade.com/311389/shawnamalcom/giada-de-laurentiis-new-restaurant-las-vegas/ (accessed December 2015).
11. Pete Wells, "You Don't Need to Tell Them Giada Sent You," *New York Times*, August 13, 2014, p. D6(L).
12. Scott Stump, "Giada on new Las Vegas restaurant: I cried in the bathroom at opening party," *Today.com*, June 3, 2014, http://www.today.com/popculture/giada-new-las-vegas-restaurant-i-cried-bathroom-opening-party-2D79749831 (accessed January 2016).

Chapter 5: Cooking for Causes

1. Lisa Hirsch, "Giada Pays Tribute to Late Brother with New PSA," *Entertainment Tonight*, April 11, 2013, http://www.etonline.com/news/132801_Giada_De_Laurentiis_Pays_Tribute_to_Late_Brother_Dino_with_New_PSA/ (accessed January 2016).

2. Robin Hilmantel, "Giada: 'Protect Yourself From Skin Cancer,'" *Women's Health*, April 2013, http://www.womenshealthmag.com/health/giada-protect-yourself-from-skin-cancer (accessed January 2016).

3. Staff writer, "Giada De Laurentiis Appears in Public Service Announcement for Stand Up To Cancer and Melanoma Research Alliance," *PR Newswire*, via Stand Up To Cancer.org, April 11, 2013, http://www.standup2cancer.org/press_release/view/giada _de_laurentiis_appears_in_new_psa_for_su2c_and_the _melanoma_research_a (accessed December 2015).

4. Hilmantel, "Giada: 'Protect Yourself From Skin Cancer.'"

5. Staff, "Giada De Laurentiis supports Alex's Lemonade Stand," Alex's Lemonade Stand Foundation YouTube channel, October 9, 2012, https://www.youtube.com/watch?v=L01Of0QEu2c (accessed December 2015).

6. Ibid.

7. Oxfam America staff, "Oxfam America announces Giada De Laurentiis as new Ambassador," Oxfamamerica.org, October 16, 2008, http://www.oxfamamerica.org/press/oxfam-america -announces-giada-de-laurentiis-as-new-ambassador / (accessed December 2015).

8. Oxfam America staff, "Giada De Laurentiis marks World Food Day with trip to Peru," Oxfamamerica.org, October 16, 2009, http:// www.oxfamamerica.org/press/giada-de-laurentiis-marks-world -food-day-with-trip-to-peru/ (accessed January 2016).

9. Lisa Kovitz, "Barilla Introduces 'The Celebrity Pasta Lovers' Cookbook' and Calls on Pasta Lovers Everywhere to Help Fight Hunger," PR Newswire, January 30, 2007, http://multivu .prnewswire.com/mnr/barilla/26618/ (accessed January 2016).

10. Food Network staff, "Giada De Laurentiis Biography," Food Network, http://www.foodnetwork.com/chefs/giada-de -laurentiis/bio.html (accessed December 2015).

11. Delinda Lombardo, "Third Annual Tiger Woods 'Block Party' Raises Over $1M," October 14, 2007, https://www.looktothestars .org/news/383-third-annual-tiger-woods-block-party-raises -over-1m (accessed December 2015).

12. Staff, "Giada De Laurentiis: Why I Ran Away From Prince William," *People*, November 3, 2013, http://www.people.com /people/article/0,,20751032,00.html (accessed December 2015).

13. PR Newswire staff, "Andrea Bocelli Honored at Star-Studded Keep Memory Alive Gala," PR Newswire, June 15, 2015, https://www .looktothestars.org/news/13832-andrea-bocelli-honored-at -star-studded-keep-memory-alive-gala (accessed January 2016).

14. Jennifer Chan, "Giada De Laurentiis Prepares for Modeling Debut at New York Fashion Week," E! Online, February 6, 2014, http:// www.eonline.com/news/508125/giada-de-laurentiis -prepares-for-modeling-debut-at-new-york-fashion -week-watch-the-video?cmpid=rss-000000-rssfeed-365 -topstories&utm_source=eonline&utm_medium=rssfeeds&utm _campaign=rss_topstories (accessed January 2016).

Chapter 6: Recipe for Becoming a Chef

1. Lori Berger, "Giada Heats Things Up!" *Redbook*, February 2011, p. 130+.

2. Brandi Chang, "Giada De Laurentiis at 2013 Angel Awards," Mingle Media TV Red Carpet Report, August 12, 2013, https:// youtu.be/4jAI7LCmJOo (accessed January 2016).

3. Ibid.

4. Staff, "Giada De Laurentiis Quotes," IMdB, http://www.imdb .com/name/nm1373094/bio?ref_=nm_dyk_qt_sm#quotes (accessed December 2015).

5. Anna Monette Roberts. "The Story You Haven't Heard About Giada De Laurentiis' Rise to Fame," *Popsugar.com*, June 29, 2014, http://www.popsugar.com/food/Story-You-Havent-Heard -About-Giada-De-Laurentiis-Rise-Fame-35078008 (accessed January 2016).

Chapter 7: Awards, Achievements, and Endorsements

1. Staff, "Jane Lynch and Giada De Laurentiis To Be Honored By Project Angel Food," Project Angel Food press release, July 19, 2013, https://www.looktothestars.org/news/10511-jane-lynch

-and-giada-de-laurentiis-to-be-honored-by-project-angel-food (accessed December 2015).

2. Ibid.

3. Kim Sayid, "Academia Barilla and Italian Chef and Author Giada De Laurentiis Launch Italian Gourmet Line," Academia Barilla press release, July 1, 2008, http://www.prweb.com /releases/academia-barilla-launches/giada-delaurentiis-line /prweb1067224.htm (accessed January 2016).

4. Chief Marketer staff, "Pyrex Cooks Up Sweeps With Chef Giada De Laurentiis," Chief Marketer, February 28, 2007, http://www .chiefmarketer.com/pyrex-cooks-up-sweeps-with-chef-giada -de-laurentiis/ (accessed December 2015).

5. Staff, "Making the Most of Celebrity Endorsement," Two/Ten Marketing, http://www.twotenagency.com/case-study/making -the-most-of-celebrity-endorsement (accessed January 2016).

6. Staff, "Target Stores in Chicago Area Receive Multiple Design Reinventions for Enhanced One-Stop Shopping," PR Newswire, October 18, 2010, http://www.prnewswire.com /news-releases/target-stores-in-chicago-area-receive -multiple-design-reinventions-for-enhanced-one-stop -shopping-105165544.html (accessed December 2015).

7. Staff, "Target Canada Announces Brands Set to Launch In Canadian Stores," January 25, 2013, https://corporate.target.com /article/2013/01/target-canada-announces-brands-to-launch-in -canadi (accessed January 2016).

8. "Target Canada Announces Brands Set to Launch in Canadian Stores," A Bullseye View (Target's YouTube channel), January 28, 2013, https://www.youtube.com/watch?v=ZxLMb5PT3P0 (accessed January 2016).

9. Staff, "What's in a name? How celebrity products rate," Consumer Reports, September 6, 2011, http://www.consumerreports.org /cro/news/2011/09/what-s-in-a-name-how-celebrity-products -rate/index.htm (accessed January 2016).

10. Staff, "Best Pasta Sauces: Find Out Which Marinara and Tomato Sauces Come out on Top on Top of Spaghetti," Consumer Reports, August 2012, http://www.consumerreports.org/cro /magazine/2012/08/best-pasta-sauces/indexad.htm (accessed January 2016).

11. Staff, "Bella Sera Wines Partner with Celebrity Chef Giada De Laurentiis to Inspire Beautiful Evenings," Bella Sera Wines, May 20, 2010, http://www.talentnewsnetwork.com/bella-sera-wines -partner-with-celebrity-chef-giada-de-laurentiis-to-inspire -beautiful-evenings/ (accessed January 2016).

12. Staff, "Bella Sera Wines and Chef Giada De Laurentiis Declare Final Call for Entries in Recipe Contest," *Food & Beverage Close-Up*, June 29, 2011.

13. Staff, "Giada De Laurentiis Is Clairol's Newest Face," *People*, May 29, 2012, http://stylenews.peoplestylewatch.com/2012/05/29 /giada-de-laurentiis-clairol-natural-instincts/ (accessed January 2016).

14. Ibid.

15. Ashley Reich, "Giada De Laurentiis Gets Real About Life Post-Divorce," Huffington Post, November 18, 2015, http://www .huffingtonpost.com/entry/giada-de-laurentiis-gets-real-about -divorce_564cc72fe4b08c74b733c3ab (accessed January 2016).

16. Staff, "Wayfair Partners with Giada De Laurentiis and Food Network on New Series Giada Entertains," Wayfair Inc. press release, December 15, 2015, http://finance.yahoo.com/news /wayfair-partners-giada-laurentiis-food-141500087.html (accessed December 2015).

17. Lori Berger, "Giada Heats Things Up!" *Redbook*, February 2011, p. 130+.

18. "Giada De Laurentiis on Life After Marriage," The Meredith Vieira Show (YouTube), November 6, 2015, https://youtu.be /yBqgQ0a6To0 (accessed January 2016).

GLOSSARY

adapted—Something that is changed to make it better suited for a purpose different from the original purpose.

amateur—A person who does something at a lesser skill level than a professional.

antipasti—Cold meat and vegetables, usually served as the first course of a large meal.

apprenticeship—A period of time when a person learns work skills while on the job.

aspiring—Describing someone who wants to achieve a certain level of success.

béchamel—(bech-A-mell) A type of rich, white sauce.

certification—An official, usually written approval that someone has reached a certain skill or knowledge level.

chopping—The act of cutting up food roughly into pieces.

culinary—Of or related to cooking.

endorsement—A public statement of support or approval.

gourmet—Fancy, special, or elaborate, with regard to food.

hospitality—The act of providing food, drinks, etc., for people who are the guests or customers of an organization.

inaugural—Happening as the first one in a series of similar events.

indulging—Allowing oneself to take part in some kind of special pleasure.

mastering—Having control of or authority over something, in particular, a task.

production—Refers to the elements involved in creating a show, film, or other artistic endeavor.

prospective—Referring to something that is likely to happen in the future.

supremes—Sections.

synonymous—Having the same meaning.

FURTHER READING

Books

De Laurentiis, Giada. *Recipe for Adventure: Naples!* New York, NY: Grosset & Dunlap, 2013.

Kezich, Tullio, and Alessandra Levantesi. *Dino: The Life and Films of Dino De Laurentiis.* New York, NY: Hyperion, 2004.

Meyer, Susan. *A Career as a Chef.* New York, NY: Rosen Publishing, 2012.

Pishner Walker, Diana. *Spaghetti and Meatballs: Growing Up Italian.* Terra Alta, WV: Headline Books, 2015.

Websites

Giada De Laurentiis

www.giadadelaurentiis.com/

Go to Giada De Laurentiis's official website for recipes, shows, books, and more.

Food Network: Giada De Laurentiis

www.foodnetwork.com/chefs/giada-de-laurentiis.html

Visit the Food Network's Giada De Laurentiis page, which includes recipes, photos, videos, bloopers, and a look behind the scenes and on set.

INDEX